IN MY OWN SHIRE

Recent Titles in
Contributions to the Study of World Literature

IN MY OWN SHIRE

Region and Belonging in British Writing, 1840–1970

Stephen Wade

Contributions to the Study of World Literature, Number 119

Westport, Connecticut
London

Library of Congress Cataloging-in-Publication Data

Wade, Stephen, 1948–

In my own shire: region and belonging in British writing, 1840–1970/Stephen Wade.
p. cm. — (Contributions to the study of world literature, ISSN 0738-9345 ; no. 119)

Includes bibliographical references (p.) and index.

ISBN 0-313-32182-5 (alk. paper)

1. English literature—20th century—History and criticism. 2. Regionalism in literature. 3. English literature—19th century—History and criticism. 4. Place (Philosophy) in literature. 5. Great Britain—In literature. 6. Group identity in literature. I. Title. II. Series.

PR478.R44 W34   2002

820.9'32—dc21   2002074912

British Library Cataloguing in Publication Data is available.

Library of Congress Catalog Card Number: 2002074912

ISBN: 0–313–32182–5
ISSN: 0738–9345

First published in 2002

Praeger Publishers, 88 Post Road West, Westport, CT 06881
An imprint of Greenwood Publishing Group, Inc.
www.praeger.com

Printed in the United States of America

The paper used in this book complies with the
Permanent Paper Standard issued by the National
Information Standards Organization (Z39.48–1984).

10 9 8 7 6 5 4 3 2 1

Copyright Acknowledgments

Extracts from James Hanley, *The Welsh Sonata* (p. 122), and from an unpublished interview with James Hanley by his son, Liam (pp. 119–120), reprinted by kind permission of Liam Hanley.

Extract from "Adestrop," by Edward Thomas (p. 84), reprinted by kind permission of Myfanwy Thomas.

In my own shire, if I was sad,
Homely comforters I had:
The earth, because my heart was sore,
Sorrowed for the son she bore.

A. E. Housman, A Shropshire Lad, XLI

Contents

Introduction

The variety of attachments to place and community we superficially label "belonging" is arguably the most elusive weasel-word in the English vocabulary. The feeling of belonging may be created by a huge ideological process or by a microcosmic network of allegiances, cash–nexus exchanges, and relationships. The question we should be asking in the literary history of regional belonging is why the concept has proved so elusive. We have rarely gone deeper than a vague notion of locality and sentimentalism in discussions of regional writing. Yet an overview of writing from the British Isles, as reflected in anthologies produced by major British publishers, such as the Norton, the Longman, or the Macmillan volumes, quickly gives us the impression of a constant interplay between metropolitan centers and regional peripheries.

The creative impulse of the regional writer complicates the idea of nationhood; but the texts from regional writers often find a place in canonical positioning, forcing us to revise the nature of the non-metropolitan stance of the writer. A useful example would be the Brontës, clearly identified as "Yorkshire" writers and now a central part of the heritage industry in that county; but they also have to be understood and placed rightly alongside (say) Dickens or Thackeray in evaluations of English fiction.

The questions addressed in this book concern the complications created by the established perspectives taken on ideas of regional identity.

In tracing the development of this writing, the study of the texts will always take note of parallels in popular culture and indeed in social and political history. Previously, critics and readers have accepted too easily the placing of the adjective "regional" before the noun "writer" and assumed that the word refers to some ill-defined area of "place" or romantic attachment to a circumscribed stratum of social community. The mythic dimension in British literary and cultural history too glibly assumes a position of authority, and the mass media create the ensuing misreadings. We seem to enjoy defining British writers by locality. Yet "region" or "province" implies a defined area separate from the metropolitan center. Hence, in cases where writers from outside London, Dublin, Edinburgh, or Cardiff have been read as Scottish, Irish, Welsh, or regional English, there have been huge simplifications in assessment. For instance, it is accepted practice to think of James Joyce as an Irish writer and to concentrate on the nature of Dublin in his work, yet in terms of a view from London, Dublin and environs may be "regional." There is a need to clarify.

There are also some clarifications required in terms of being sure what varieties of regional consciousness may be identified. In British culture, the notion just will not go away, and what we see so clearly in art and literature is continually obfuscated by political and economic issues. In the course of one weekend in February 2001, the newspapers carried stories on "Chancellor Backs English Devolution," "Northern Cities Try Hard Sell in South," and "The Poetic, Patriotic and Proud Welsh," and they presented a list of websites concerned with the North–South divide. These all involved emotional statements about belonging, and in most cases the belonging was to idealistic and historical instances. Appeals were made to stereotypes, to the land, to song and poetry; nothing has changed since the 1840s debates on the north and the location of industry.

"Belonging" as a concept in literature and culture may be detectable in a number of manifestations. My history includes these commonly found categories:

1. the creation of the center–periphery duality;
2. the challenges to the pastoral genre and agrarian reality;
3. the new consciousness in writing after the emergence of the new cities;

4. duality in both nationhood and self;

5. the relation of locality to region.

In terms of historical context, there are almost infinite possibilities if the literary historian looks at the impact of social and demographic change on writing. A typically complex case study could be made of Mrs. Gaskell's Manchester, for instance. Between 1821 and 1841, the population of Manchester had grown by over 40 percent.[1] As Engels's survey of the city had shown, there was a clear split between the villas of the factory owners and the jerry-built houses and cellars of the proletariat. When Gaskell describes the Davenport family, suffering and dying in their squalid basement, we are aware of the social geography inherent in their pain and that economic forces, opposed to those in focus in the hands of the novelist, are at work. Our reading of *North and South* is always incomplete without an awareness that the book was written just before the emergence of Manchester as a city of immense cultural achievement and civic pride. How different is the city in 1870, when the first unregulated flood of immigrant labor had been settled and absorbed more rationally!

There is also the noted variation in the nature of the new Victorian cities. Sheffield and Birmingham had an industrial structure that was organized largely by small units of masters and apprentices, whereas Manchester and Leeds had mostly huge mills and factories, with a large unskilled or semiskilled labor force under an authoritarian management. Therefore, the regional sense would be expected to be more diverse in expression according to the newer feelings of community or otherwise. It is doubtful that a poorly paid largely immigrant proletariat would feel an allegiance to Lancashire or to Yorkshire. What organizational Yorkshire provincial sense had existed before the nineteenth century was only in the context of the wealthy classes, as in the Yorkshire association formed by Christopher Wyvill in 1779.

Of the areas of interest listed above, perhaps the most problematic is that of the identity split; in a recent debate about R. L. Stevenson's novel, *Dr. Jekyll and Mr. Hyde,* Andrew O'Hagan made the point that the novel is one of the best expositions of the schism in Scottish identity created by what he termed "the culture of 'Nevertheless . . .'"[2]—that is, the uncertainty of what being Scottish is. After all, Scottish identity had been made prominent again in cultural discussion, since the massive influence of Walter Scott and the growth of Scottish versions of Romanticism, and the culture industry had burgeoned, by way of Queen Victoria's love of the Highlands and Landseer's paintings.[3]

In the context of England and Englishness, the notion of region and belonging becomes clouded by such phenomena as the profusion of neo-Romantic writing at the end of the nineteenth century and into the years of Georgian poetry. But there are aspects of English writing in this sense that have still not reached a central position in our understanding of the provincial attitude to literature. Too often, the notion of place has been exemplified in songs such as William Barnes's *Linden Lea* or in poems such as Edward Thomas's "Adlestrop." This only serves to perpetuate the media construction of the "English idyll," which is often appropriated by those who wish to sell ideas and goods by the ideology of regional belonging—in this case, the boundary between love of place and the "local" on the one hand, and the idealization of a specific area in opposition to the "foreign" or "distant" on the other.

My inquiry is also concerned with those more dominant and influential strands of British writing that link to harsh social history. It is difficult to interpret the regional novels of the Victorian period, for instance, without incorporating a discussion of the fascinating interrelationship of class and region. It is hard to deny the tendency of writers to "explain" the provincial to Londoners (or to targeted readerships), as Arnold Bennett illustrates in the opening of his first novel, *A Man from the North*:

There grows in the north country a certain kind of youth of whom it may be said that he was born to be a Londoner. The metropolis, and everything that appertains to it, has for him an imperious fascination. Long before schooldays are over he learns to take a doleful pleasure in watching the exit of the London train.[4]

Here, Bennett is explaining the pull of London, but in doing so he opens the provincial mind-set to inspection. What muddies the water—and will continue to do so—is the suburban origins. The proliferation of the English suburbanite adds a new dimension to the chronicle of the region-and-belonging phenomenon. As the story advances, it becomes clear that the "man from the north" may be vaguely northern, whatever that means, but he is primarily suburban. The term "provincial" used pejoratively may well have its roots in the criticism based on those inhabiting the no-man's-land between the metropolitan and the truly rural.

Once an inquiry is made into the nature of that peculiarly English version of regional belonging, all kinds of emotional attachments are revealed. If A. E. Housman's "Shropshire" is—as I argue in chapter 4—a construct rather clumsily mixing childhood idylls with a long eulogy to the typically rural English shire, then it surely explains why the phenomenal success of *A Shropshire Lad* has been largely in terms of the enduring myth of the "Golden World." It is not very different from Duke Senior's forest kingdom in *As You Like It*—a successful blend of dreamy escapism and the dark shadow of modernity:

Oliver: Where will the old Duke live?

Charles: They say he is already in the Forest of Arden, and a many merry men with him; and there they live like the old Robin Hood of England. They say many young gentlemen flock to him every day, and fleet the time carelessly as they did in the Golden World.[5]

The "modernity" in Housman tends to be war or the city; for Shakespeare it was more to be located in the idea of sophistication and mendacity in corrupt court individuals. The myth of the "Golden World" persists in regional belonging, and much of the writing studied in my survey has no difficulty in melding myth and reality.

What, then, are the definite centers of interest in all this confusion? My argument suggests that there are three fundamental themes that intermingle constantly: first, the idea of "home and away," second, the need to find certainties in one's locality, and, finally, the creative binary of past and present identity. A perfect example of all these coming together is in Housman's poem XLI in *A Shropshire Lad*. Here, the contrast of London and "my own shire" is made simplistically, in terms first of close community and common support, then of the inherent beauty of nature, and, finally, of the developed idea of the "mortal sickness of the mind" created in London. Consequently, the regional is healthy, understandable, communal, and unchanging, as in Duke Senior's forest or in the Victorian market-town communities in the notably successful *Our Village* (1832) by Mary Mitford and *Cranford* (1851) by Elizabeth Gaskell.

The point here is that these successes all relate to the pull of domesticity within a circumscribed locality. The regional belonging so prominent in British writing is invariably of a piece with the vision of humanity that sees happiness and virtue in the microcosm: the known world and the community bonds within it.

Clearly, any study of regional writing in this period also has to turn to broad political change, because much in class structure, democracy, industrial relations, and the location of industry ultimately affected, or indeed created, "regional" identity as it came to be seen by the end of the nineteenth century. There is a clear source for the dialect almanacs that developed from ca. 1850, for example: the gradual education of the artisan class and the new cultured middle class with time for libraries and philosophical societies. For instance, *The Clock Almanac*, started by John Hartley in 1866, constructed a working-class sensibility that was largely absent from mainline fiction at the time. In contrast, the more literate and intertextual *Saunterer's Satchel* of James Burnley (based in Bradford) clearly had the lawyers, teachers, and managers of that city in mind. But the point is that behind these local celebrations of regional difference lies the list of stepping-stones toward the creation of a new readership for literature: from the Reform Act of 1868, the Education Act of 1870, and the first proper union for the artisans, the Amalgamated Society of Engineers (1851), the impact on regional consciousness was immense.

The interest in local dialect is indicative of this quiet revolution in writing and local readership. There had always been presses catering for the working man, from almanacs to broadsheet ballads and chapbooks, and the circulating libraries had catered for middle-class taste in novels and improving literature; but the arrival of dialect writing confirmed regional belonging as a central Victorian cultural feature. The remarkable proliferation of printed ephemera conveying humorous verse and narrative was accompanied by the "Penny Readings" for the working man, and stars were made on the reading circuit—men like Edwin Waugh, who "earned money from his published work and later from giving dialect readings of his work within and beyond Lancashire."[6]

From the middle of the century, the English Dialect Society had begun its series of regional dialect glossaries, and in 1897 the Yorkshire Dialect Society was founded. It is clear that dialect writing illustrates these qualities of sentimentality, home, past and present, and Golden Land myth; indeed, in many columns of local newspapers today, the dialect humor column still holds a place. At one level, the dialect writing in the almanacs and readings was a defense of what Percy Grainger would have called "blue-eyed English" against the consolidation of Standard English grammar in the new Revised Code emanating from the 1870 Education Act (the one that created Tess Durbeyfield as a good citizen). But on a more elemental level, it is a Canute-like facing of the sea of change. Regional belonging has often been limited to this, but it is hard to overlook the mechanism by which a writer uses the particular and visible in order to locate the general ills of a society or a pervading ideology. In fact, regional writing tends to follow a method not unlike 1950s science fiction, in which the writer created a manageably explicable world, a microcosm, and then placed it within a larger, threatening "other": an alien element bringing disruption or ruin.

One of the persisting foregrounding methods of regional writing is what might be called the "Farfrae" effect: in Hardy's *The Mayor of Casterbridge* (1866), the Scot Donald Farfrae—"from far away," literally—is at once a creative and a disruptive force, providing the oppositional factor in the main plot. Hardy often makes effective use of the "stranger," of course, and he makes his regional selfhood the combative factor with the well-traveled stranger. His microcosmic fictional Wessex could be a metaphor for the regional implosive conflicts at the heart of much successful fictional exploration of the diversity of the English identity.

Moving into the twentieth century, A. J. P. Taylor noted that in the 1920s, "There was a fairly clear line between north and south . . . though one would hardly guess it from most works of literature or political history."[7] Certainly, it was not until the 1930s that regional writing took on a new urgency in the eyes of the literary establishment. When Phyllis Bentley wrote a monograph for PEN in 1941, she commented that overseas readers would find in English writing an amazing diversity and that "The potential difference between two human habitations must not be measured in mere mileage distance alone . . . but by 'basic human communication time.'"[8] She goes on to explain the comparative sense of historical perspective that different nations place on each other. In other words, the book shows a demand for the regional novel (in that instance) to be placed in terms of broader perspectives: it had won a new respect, and F. R. Leavis was to struggle to find a place for the Brontës in his seminal *The Great Tradition* (1948). He did not do so, but they had to be argued out.

The 1930s and 1940s add a new strand to the history in the following pages. The concept of documentary fiction became inextricably bound up with the regions. Modernism had already introduced the revisionary thinking about country and city, center and periphery, outstandingly in Joyce's work, but now the journeys into the "other England" undertaken by writers such as J. B. Priestley and George Orwell, together with the advent of the documentary film and later Mass Observation, made the regions a wholly new expanse of "material" for the writer. The North–South divide and the communities around the various coalfields provided the notion of regional belonging with a hard viewpoint of selfhood and relationships within poverty. Some of the regions appeared to be as distant from London as parts of Africa, and in fact some of the documentary writing of that period has the tone of Conrad's *Heart of Darkness*.

Philip Massey wrote a study of a community in Ebbw Fach, South Wales—an issue of *Fact* magazine for November 1937—and the survey is introduced with this manifesto: "Those who read our editorial in no. 4 will recall that we announced then the beginning of an attempt to survey typical corners of Britain as truthfully and as penetratingly as if our investigators had been inspecting an African village."[9] Regional belonging by 1940 often meant mere survival on the bread or poverty line, and the old myths of community and home took on a new, significant pattern of meanings.

The final phase of regional writing covered here is perhaps the most vibrant and notable of all: the era of the regional novel in the 1940–1960 period is rich in discoveries and reappraisals. In this section, I start with James Hanley and end with the Liverpool poets. But perhaps, despite the popularity of the Northern novel in the hands of John Braine, Stan Barstow, and David Storey, there is something just as profound and consequential in the developments in nonmetropolitan poetry in that period. I end with the first published collections of Hughes and Heaney, but before that—as Hans-Werner Ludwig and Lothar Fietz have shown in their important collection, *Poetry in the British Isles: Non-Metropolitan Perspectives* (1995)—there are major figures and topics in need of due cognizance here: MacDiarmid in Scotland, the generation of Anglo–Welsh poets around Dylan Thomas in Wales, revisionary thinking on the poetry of place, and, of course, the burgeoning Anglo–Irish scene, with figures such as Kavanagh at its center.

In fact, the influence on the modern British novel and on poetry from the periphery has been cyclical, with important figures forcing us to rethink the image of the region, interspersed with more bland and monolithic stages of writing in between. For instance, in fiction,

Braine's *Room at the Top* (1957), Alan Sillitoe's *Saturday Night and Sunday Morning* (1958), and Stan Barstow's *A Kind of Loving* (1960) undoubtedly turned readers to the Midlands and the north to see a new vibrancy, rebellion, and unrest, but it was the poetry of the time that went deeper into the actual nature of regional belonging. In Philip Larkin's collection, *The Whitsun Weddings* (1960), for instance, poems like "Large Cool Store" and "Here" give far more profound observations of difference than much of the working-class fiction.

The poetry of working-class writers obviously widened the potential range of subjects and themes in regional writing, but much of the critical interest has been in linguistic experiment and subcultural explication. The sense of place is the abiding, unchanging steady center of regional writing. My history starts with Gaskell's Manchester and ends with McGough's Liverpool; but, undeniably, the impact of Ireland on English writers provides an entirely separate piece of literary history—hard to trace with any certainty, but a presence nevertheless. Writing in English in Wales and Scotland may have been less influential, but each body of writing has made a borderland of the mind as sure and meaningful as anything in Kavanagh or Heaney. Ironically, the common ground between the first text we look at and the last is Ireland—at least in origins. What the Victorians would have called "the Celtic fringe" has persisted and been a powerful force for renewal in English regional writing, and the persistence of the English rural idyll, the Housman-centered longing for stasis, has found new tributaries as the main rivers have dried up.

It may be that the conflict between being English and being from a certain "shire" or county may always have the element of unease that John Lucas noted:

Regionalism could offer itself as an alternative to the concept of Englishness that required a person to identify with the monarchy, the church, and all those structure of the state which upheld liberty for some. "Nation heere! Nation theere! I'm a man and yo're another, but nation's nowheere." The words are spoken by Daniel Robson in Elizabeth Gaskell's *Sylvia's Lovers.*[10]

With all these wider questions in mind, we might ask: what, then, was the point at which regional consciousness found a prominent place in British writing? Even more specific to this book, what elements of influence from intellectual and cultural history caused the dynamic

impulse of writing about territory, difference, and community so noticeable in the Victorian regional novel?

One obvious answer would be the advent of the railways and communication in the late-Victorian period. By 1860, railways had brought the
provinces nearer but also made their differences more easily defined. It
could also be added that centralization and standardization in all its
forms impinged on the creative arts generally, and so, by means of an
existential act, writers insisted on their differences from the norms by
means of reference to their individuality. To put the case rather force-
fully, if *home* was supposed to be a distant community of loosely
aligned areas of a huge metropolis, much in the sense that an *alma
mater* was a home, then what was the real "home" in contrast?

In 1964, the historian Donald Read wrote a history of the English
provinces, and in his closing chapters he surveyed the position of the
arts with regard to centralization. He was writing at the time of the
rediscovery of Northern writing, and he refers to Rayner Heppenstall's
essay on the subject, noting that "Dylan Thomas is . . . our last writer to
draw strength from a living provincial background."[11] Read insists that
there is still "individuality" in the writing from such places as Salford,
Nottingham, and Bingley at that time. The interesting point about this
discussion is that it is set in the context of Matthew Arnold's denigration
of the "provincial" as opposed to the metropolitan. The revision of
Arnoldian ideas had been more than dismissed by this point in cultural
history. The fact that my survey ends with this points to the significance
of that profound challenge to the metropolitan center that has taken
place in the last few decades of the twentieth century.

1

The Inheritance:
Past and Present

Looking for the roots of regional writing as foundations for the literature of the second half of the nineteenth century involves unraveling a literary complexity. On the surface, it would be obvious to point to Maria Edgeworth and Walter Scott, as they defined particular versions of Britishness in relative terms. But the fact is that around 1840, what had been established as the writing of a specific region of Britain was a multilayered concept, depending on whether you looked at the situation from London, Dublin, Edinburgh, or Cardiff.

This concept embraced the various traditions of pastoral and elegiac writing insofar as these projected ideals onto named localities. It also covers the poetry of Robert Bloomfield and Clare, the "peasant-poet" genre, and, lastly, the elements of Romanticism found in Wordsworth's celebration of place. But here, in his early Cumberland poems, the waters become muddy: his attempts to write a simple, folk-centered series of narratives impinge on earlier traditions, reaching back to Gray's meditations and even the balladry of Percy's *Reliques* (1765).

The confluence of these disparate sources impacts on the kind of knowingly regional writing in the literary construction of what is defined as a "knowable community," and it is interesting to note that, from the early Victorian period through to recent years, the parallel genre of local autobiography has always thrived. In beginning this survey with the decade that saw the publication of Elizabeth Gaskell's *North and*

South, Emily Brontë's *Wuthering Heights,* and Charlotte Brontë's *Jane Eyre*, the fact of industrialization and the process of relentless enclosure is always a basis for change, and the writing reacts to this. The springboard for much regional writing in the 1840s was a challenge: how to fuse the established Romantic modes of writing in opposition to ideas of nationhood and demographic flux with the new discovery of the individual self. Combined with this is the tendency of regional writing to challenge the cultural assumptions of the metropolitan center.

The source texts and potential categories of writing involved in answering the question about what influenced these first truly regional novels are about place both as common ground and of personal biographical significance. But the method adopted in this book is to examine representative texts that specifically created imagined communities and made a defined region a literary invention. There is a clear line in nineteenth-century writing tracing the development of areas and places as literary inventions, and although it could be argued that the emergence of the novel was always going to be "regional" in the sense of the writer providing a circumscribed community, the regional in the present sense has to extend this to a visionary, mythic plane. Therefore, while Dickens's Coketown in *Hard Times* is a "region" in the sense that it is a documented Lancashire setting and we can follow Dickens's research and his three weeks spent in Preston, the result is not an integrated vision with a realistic base: it is melodrama grafted onto a composite working-class community that could be any northern English industrial town.

In the latter sense, the regional novels in the nineteenth century are represented by Gaskell's *North and South*, Eliot's *Middlemarch*, Hardy's Wessex fiction, and Bennett's Clayhanger series. The poetry in the same period could be similarly traced, as could the biographical prose. But in terms of the Romantic basis for this, the starting point is in the notions of place and community as established by the immensely influential writers, Scott, Wordsworth, Burns, and Clare, and by the folklorists and ballad collectors.

This work is located in terms of these characteristics: the idea of place, historical–present axis, natural landscape, man-made landscape, and linguistic–social conventions. These elements explain Scott's phenomenal success in the Waverley Novels, of course. Being published a century after the Act of Union that united England and Scotland (1707), these construct, through historical romance, a profound descriptive index of Scottishness—a sense of difference formed by character, environment, and social-relational functions in the family and kinship of both Highlands and Lowlands. In rooting many of these writings in the Borders, Scott enlarges on the folk traditions and imposes his own fascinations with chivalry, militarism, and idealized courtly love onto a fabric of basic social realism, notably in the characters in the working-class sectors.

Scott's Waverley Novels had established more than the historical regional novel; they had made it acceptable for a novelist to people a mythic literary framework with a notably separate Scottish identity. This identity Scott defines through language, custom, dress, social structure, and imagination. The physical environment is present, but the attention is always to the interaction between the individual and the communal forces he or she must comprehend. As a lawyer–novelist, Scott naturally took an interest in the power nexus, and thus his novels, whatever else they do in terms of historiography, focus on an individual imagination in a context of constraint. But the place and its social fabric shape the heroes just as profoundly as the narrating selves of Wordsworth's poems.

It is not difficult to find deeper levels of interest that make the Waverley Novels such an effective template for understanding what came later in the genre. As with Edgeworth's *Castle Rackrent* (1800), Scott feels it necessary to inject that element of anecdote, wayward humor, and local mythology so necessary to fiction that needs to show a difference, a plane of being on the cultural periphery. A novel such as *The Heart of Midlothian,* for instance, has the leisurely storycraft of the historian as raconteur, elaborating on the differences between, for example, London's Tyburn and Edinburgh's Grass Market. The third chapter of the novel uses these differences in order to introduce the Porteous riots, and from there we have a series of explanations, in the actions of the mob, as to the varieties of morality present in the community. He chooses a community under pressure and against the law, and he makes Edinburgh a significant part of the sequence of chapters in which Porteous is dragged from jail to be executed.

The relation between the poetry of Wordsworth and Clare, on the one hand, and the general notion of regional writing, on the other, lies in the assertion that varieties of knowledge are circumscribed. For Clare, Helpston and the Fens are knowable through a grammar of nature in which birdsong, botany, and fieldwork form the integuments of being.

Wordsworth may have insisted on the certainty of feeling and imagination as ways of finding personal existential comfort, but again he names places and records times. This indicates a sense of place being a force for opening up sensibility and consciousness. One element in later regional writing was this need to create a sense of individual learning and growing in the setting of a known, familiar place.

This is not to say that their poetic landscapes are devoid of people. Wordsworth needed to introduce workers and travelers; Clare's poetry is never far from the human center of meaning. Also, in Robert Burns and the "peasant poet" tradition we have a feeling of labor within a quasi-pastoral setting, but the key to its success is the vision of a warm, bonded community within the idyll.

All this helps to answer the questions about why and how a regional perspective came into prominence in British writing of the Victorian period. Prose writing of several categories mixed in this development, but the core of the present study is the analysis of how and why the need to invent imaginative regions happened and why it has had such a profound effect on ideas of nation, Englishness, and the border identities of Anglo–Welsh, Anglo–Irish, and Anglo–Scottish writing. A useful first step is to focus on the link between the local and the regional. In an age in which social change was accelerating and traditional communities felt the first shock of modernity, writers and readers wanted to be reminded of the definition of community as a human microcosm, close and physical, expressing a version of Clare's intimate knowledge of Swordy Well or Wordsworth's feeling about Grasmere. Ronald Blythe has written extensively about this trait in John Clare, for instance, explaining the allegiance to place in this way:

To be a native once meant to be a born thrall. Clare's enthralment by Helpston presents the indigenous eye at its purest, at its most naturally disciplined and at its most informed. By his extraordinary ability to see furthest when the view was strictly limited, he was able to develop a range of perception which outstripped the most accomplished and travelled commentary on landscape.[1]

Naturally, these areas of human imagination often reflect a myth that sustains a region's sense of itself. The overlapping terms region and nation add to the issue here. But whatever patterns of meaning we wish to impose on a region and our belonging as a construct of this, notions of ideology will never be far away. In the local–regional interface this may be clearly seen. Writers tend to prefer a demarcated area, a special limitation in which their forms and plots will blossom. Inevitably, this involves a juxtaposition of the private and public lives of characters; in this way, the workings of ideology become more transparent in a local context than in an ambitious, more abstract, and generalizing work. The simplest illustration of this is in the folk literature and dialect writing of Yorkshire and Lancashire in the mid- to late-Victorian years. Here, poems and stories in the almanacs and slim volumes and songs could summarize great historical or political processes into an individual experience.

Even a cursory reading of the major Romantic writers on place and local identity provides a reminder that they were forced to negotiate meanings about a previously ignored subject: the working people. As has often been asked: where are the characters in eighteenth-century fiction who exemplify any kind of serious representation of the worker? In Austen they are shadowy figures; in the picaresque they are there to provide humor, often in caricature and slapstick; in the poetry of meditation and rural life they are still stuck in the moribund pastoral as Baucis and Philemon.

However, as Wordsworth, Burns, Clare, and Scott incorporated the landless class and figures such as farm workers, discharged soldiers, ostlers, craftsmen, and vagrants in their work, they also initiated an element of later regional writing that provided an oppositional force to the aristocratic subject and the obsession with land and ownership. In fact, in Maria Edgeworth's *Castle Rackrent* we have a succession of incompetent wastrels and adventurers in aristocratic society, and their tales are told by the servant, old Thady. Thady's narrative places the reader clearly in the eighteenth-century comic tradition of Sheridan's theater and Fielding's open road, with young bucks and old rakes indulging in duels and love matches, moving from London to Bath. But the tone of address through Thady's storytelling when the scene shifts from London to Ireland invites some pertinent judgments about the center and periphery, and the causes of local neglect as well as the explanations of local attraction.

There is also the springboard of oral and local tradition lying behind Victorian regional writing. It is difficult to overlook the presence of the pan-European discovery of "the Folk," expressed in Herder's intellectual research into folk song, Schiller's dramas, and the Grimms' fairy tales. In Britain, Percy's *Reliques* and Wilson's *Tales of the Borders* are similar phenomena, the former having been a deep influence on Scott. This was a gradual realization that whole series of narratives in poetry, song, and ancestral memory and oral form are grounded in local consciousness. The impact of this movement may be seen in a variety of texts, from Scott through Hardy's *Wessex Tales* to the Mersey poets' use of street language in the 1970s.

Arguably, the sources of nineteenth-century regional writing are a series of counterbalancing factors: the picturesque and the pastoral conventions causing a response of writing that provides a salutary reality, and then the rhetorical, highly stylized ballad impacts on Wordsworth and Coleridge, as may be clearly seen in *The Idiot Boy*. When Wordsworth challenged the diction of the previous generation's poetry in his Preface to the *Lyrical Ballads* (1798), his desire to use the language of ordinary people had a firm relation to the impetus behind the *Volkliteratur* of German writers and critics as they looked for local songs and stories in the second half of the eighteenth century. Peter Burke has explained why there was such an awakening interest in "folk": "There were thus good literary and political reasons for European intellectuals to discover popular culture when they did. However, the discovery might have remained purely literary had it not been for an older tradition of interest in manners and customs, an antiquarian tradition which goes back to the Renaissance."[2] With this in mind, it comes as no surprise than Clare's first collection was called *Poems Descriptive of Rural Life and Scenery*, and that many local dignitaries added their name to the subscription list. The fact is that "regional" was still a word that suggested the quaint and therefore implied something novel, something usually in need of patronage, and something that would provide entertainment or diversion very much in the manner of the "rude mechanicals" and their play in *A Midsummer Night's Dream*.

The "regional" has always meant an artistic invention, often when political process had tended to destroy certain feelings of difference. After the relentless highland clearances in Scotland throughout the eighteenth and nineteenth centuries, when thousands of Highlanders had gone to Canada and America, writers imagined "the Highlands" as a place in the mind, an invention of a new type of idyllic simplicity, full of strong heroic men and devoted wives who sang sweet songs as they worked. Equally, nostalgia has never been adequate to describe or explain these imaginings. They have always been tinged with those twin impulses of the national fascination with the past: guilt and loss.

Yet, around 1840, regions were either defined, circumscribed identities vaguely constructed, or definite *chronotopes* with a powerful autobiographical impulse in the writer's responses. This is an ideal point at which to introduce the chronotope, as it is a concept of vital importance to the imaginative invention of place and region. The concept comes from the theorist, Mikhail Bakhtin, who defines it in this way: "In the literary artistic chronotope, spatial and temporal indicators are fused into one carefully thought-out, concrete whole. Time, as it were, thickens, takes on flesh, becomes artistically visible; likewise, space becomes charged and responsive to the movements of time, plot and history. This intersection of axes and fusion of indicators characterizes the artistic chronotope."[3]

This is clearly relevant to that entire complex of constructions of "place" that we find in Romantic literature, and again in Modernism; it can relate to such styles as the Joycean epiphany yet also to Clare's and Wordsworth's insistence on the numinous in nature. The social history is a useful reference point for determining why this sense of place as a chronotope arrived. Once open land was enclosed, mapped, exploited, and assimilated into the political demography of the age, an invented "region" was a natural and understandable construct. That invented region had to be, by its very definition, a mystery—something to be described and to be made through narrative but essentially beyond full comprehension. John Clare used to delight in finding in his local topography deserted niches, untouched by others, and there he would read and compose his lines. The chronotope provides the critic with a template for that attempt, in Romanticism, to impose a mystery through a need to impose a numinous meaning on place.

Bakhtin finds in the chronotope something that defines and explains genres, and its usefulness in applications to regional writing is explained by Simon Trezise in an article on Thomas Hardy. Trezise notes that "the experience of a place is unique" and that in Goethe's writings on Italy we have an example of the imaginative explanation of the chronotope: "When Goethe describes Sicily as 'that miraculous centre upon which so many radii of world history converge' he provides an image of time in space: reading the contours of place is also simultaneously reading the events that happened there."[4]

With this in mind, it becomes more difficult to see the nature of the *regional* as a concept more clearly, as at one level it is a version of fantasy, imposing a construct of the individual imagination onto a social fabric. In this way the charge of sentimentality has often been put against such writing, as criticisms of the Scottish Kailyard school of the 1890s show. It is also easy to see the issue of realism as against sentimentality in the West Riding dialect poetry of the later nineteenth century. In fact, the various versions of sentimentality and melodrama, which are potentially explicable with realism as a criterion, are found as aspects of the criticism of many varieties of regional writing. This is perhaps because the effort to extend the realistic texture of life in a specific place into a self-generated fantasy is present in several genres, from pastoral poetry to the family saga.

These nonrealistic modes are partly explained by the tendency for locality to be ideologically opposed to the dominant macroeconomic functions and ideologies of the time. The human qualities such as compassion, sharing sympathy, and affection are clustered around the representations of the imagined communities of local writing. The notion of the anonymity of the individual worker, for instance, was emerging in the new towns and the factory-based industries, so it is a natural consequence of this that the general literary satirical impulse to build a critique of these social trends should be visible in local and regional writing. An example is Dickens's well documented criticism of utilitarian teaching methods in Gradgrind's school in *Hard Times*, and also his ironic use of the terms "hands" as a meiosis for human beings in the factories.

Something about the Romantic celebration of place enables a deeper layer of meaning to be discerned as the literary inventions become more complex in, for instance, the "social problem" novels of the 1840s, in which social criticism, localism, and romance are interfused. This deeper level is primarily concerned with language: the local accents and dialects of the regional tradition in the novel, for example, always have the fabric of speech deftly integrated into the other fictional elements. In Gaskell, the Brontës, Bennett, Hardy, Rogers, Scott, Eliot, and Carleton, local speech is sometimes a tool for fashioning a level of character differentiation that has to avoid the stereotypes of such features as "stage Irish" or "Mummerset." Arguably, the regional writer stands or falls according to the authenticity of the dialogue, and indeed of the nonstandard English actually integral to the narrative voice (notably prominent in *Lorna Doone,* for instance). In fact, Blackmore consciously reflects on this, imprinting through language a unique local sensual perception of experience, as in the long passage on fighting in the opening chapter. This is typified by explaining the "winkey":

The scholar obtains, by prayer or price, a handful of saltpetre, and then with the knife, wherewith he should rather be trying to mend his pens, what does he do but scoop a hole where the desk is some three inches thick. . . . Let him fill it with saltpetre, and save a little space, where the boss of the wood is . . . it will be better if he sticks the end of his candle of tallow, or rat's tail as we called it.[5]

This shows the attempt to fuse authentic local vocabulary and anecdotal style with the imagined place; such a tendency is a crux of critical debate in later regional writing, from Synge to MacDiarmid.

This bedrock of Romanticism, then, as a feature on which the regional writing of the Victorian period flourished, is an amalgam of personal expression, ideology, and innovative writing. When the second-wave Romantics, such as Browning and Tennyson, wanted to try speech features that were not standard poetic diction, as in the dramatic monologues or in Tennyson's ventures into dialect writing, they were left with a difficulty in appreciating the regional consciousness with any substance. This was intensified by the fact that Victorian determinism reached into all the arts. In the social context, this determinism meant that stereotypes of regional representation were there to be challenged by the more talented and original authors. Oscar Wilde exemplifies this, as Declan Kiberd emphasizes in his discussion of Irish stereotypes:

For Wilde sensed that antithesis was the master-key to the Victorian mind, which delighted in absolute distinctions between men and women, good and evil, English and Irish and so on. . . . The belief that the Irishman was the prisoner of heredity, diet and climate, like the conviction that a woman is by nature docile, subservient and deferential, were twin attributes of Victorian determinism. . . . The very plot of Wilde's *The Importance of Being Earnest* is an example of a determinism so extreme as to render the concept idiotic and banal.[6]

Writing locality into an imaginary dimension and making it represent features and qualities of uniqueness inevitably invites the creation of grand-scale rhetoric, hyperbole, or sheer unabashed melodrama. A central theme of any history of this genre has to be the issue of realism and the extent to which the regional overlaps with genres such as romance and popular crime, or even autobiography. The fact is that the Romantic movement established new modes of writing about place and belonging. The manifestos, such as the preface to *Lyrical Ballads*, and the poetic statements of Romantic aesthetics such as Keats's letters or *Endymion* all point to a demand for a revisionary look at the relationships involved in such concepts as nation, land, province, region, and border.

The texts that may be seen as basal, foundation texts for Victorian writers, the poets and novelists they read and were influenced by, although they were not slavishly copied, point in the direction of placing the imagination with "a local habitation and a name," because in a world in which locality was a challenged concept and the neighborhood was under threat, the act of imagining a region meant that it was possible to assert or revisit a desired human center in a materialistic society.

Yet, beneath all the theory and speculation, there is a common ground: the sense of the past, whether perceived through romance or epic, pastoral poem or ghostly tale. Scott is the reclaimer par excellence in this preoccupation with the attempt to dredge meanings from layers of history, as Peter Burke explains:

The popular culture of the years around 1800 were found just in time, or so the discoverers thought. The theme of a vanishing culture which must be recorded before it is too late recurs in their writings. . . . Sir Walter Scott declared that he collected border ballads in order to "contribute somewhat to the history of my native country; the peculiar features of whose manners are daily melting and dissolving". He believed that his contemporaries were listening to the lay of the last minstrel.[7]

2

Place and People Revealed, 1840–1860

The year 1840 has several varieties of resonance for us, looking back to a time in which Romanticism was being absorbed by artists and critics and the entire landscape of Britain was changing radically. The 1840s have become dominated in literary historiography by the "social problem" novel and the Chartist–Reformist movements percolating into working-class writing. But it was a decade that saw the emergence of the Brontës in Yorkshire, Edwin Waugh in Lancashire, and William Carleton's fiction in Ireland, and the time when the Blue Books of 1847 noted the influence of Welsh as a factor in general dissent in Wales.

Across the two decades from 1840 to 1860, there is a shift from the novels crusading against repression and poverty in the industrial north to a more consistently imagined sense of region. For instance, Scott's novels showed Emily Brontë the mechanisms of establishing a region through a mythology of place and a rhetoric of the numinous in man's spiritual longings. But Brontë's Yorkshire was extended poetically; by 1860, George Borrow was building on the platform of using Wales as a focus of the picturesque by taking it into a travel literature that depended on the human community as much as on Tintern Abbey or Snowdon.

These twenty years saw the publication of a series of key texts in the formation of that specific literature of regional imagining that was to culminate at the end of the century in the work of Hardy, Jefferies, and Bennett. In order to understand how Wessex emerged, it is necessary to isolate the various streams of genres that form the confluence of the heightened realism of the regional writing that later came to be so popular. The major texts in this sense are Gaskell's *Cranford* (first published in *Household Words* in 1851); Carleton's *Traits and Stories of the Irish Peasantry* (1842–1844); Edwin Waugh's dialect poetry of the 1840s, and George Borrow's *Wild Wales* (1862). If London is excluded (in Dickens), it is only because of the contention that center and periphery are important concepts in the creation of an imagined place and people; but, of course, a theme of Dickens's work, forming a spine throughout his oeuvre, is the oppositional interplay of self and society through home and work. Mr. Wemmick in *Great Expectations,* for instance, leaves work, goes over the river, and enters his castle (complete with drawbridge).

The clash of individuality and social determinism becomes acute in this period, and a study of the above central texts reveals more complexity in regional belonging than one might find in a cursory reading of popular regional fiction: the locally significant becomes more than a setting for departures and adventures. The historical context explains much of the focus on the regional in early Victorian writing. First, the demographic change had been staggeringly rapid and radical. Mrs. Gaskell's Manchester is a place in which the villas of the wealthy are but a short walk from the hovels of the immigrant workforce, Dickens's pitiable "hands" in his Coketown. But at the same time Edwin Waugh recites his poems of poverty and work in Manchester's literary clubs.

The aim here is to place together writings that would normally be compartmentalized for structural reasons. At times the perspective appears to be that of discerning various attempts to construct an imagined "North Country" or "Peasant's Ireland," and by 1840 these were becoming so entrenched in the popular media that there was danger of parody becoming the norm. Indeed, the "Stage Irishman," an extension of the "navvy" of the Punch cartoons and the caricatures of Irishmen from Shakespeare's Macmorris to Goldsmith's Sir Lucius O'Trigger, gave serious novelists such as William Carleton a great deal to do in order to bring some reality to bear on representation. But paradoxically, as John Sutherland quotes: "On the eve of the Victorian period a writer in the Athenaeum (28 May 1836) noted that regionalism as a theme for fiction was exhausted." Sutherland goes on to note that the Brontës, Gaskell, and George Eliot were exceptions, and that the 1851 Census reflects the changes beneath this: that "for the first time more people were living in urban rather than rural situations."[1]

This applies only if one considers the novel itself, and also the novel as regional only if it deals with place as people, as Scott had done. New varieties and subgenres were emerging, and it is useful at this point to summarize what these were.

CRANFORD AND "LOCAL" WRITING

First, there was the provincial community as an ideological mechanism for dealing with accelerated change. In this period, Elizabeth Gaskell's *Cranford* and its forebear, Mary Russell Mitford's *Our Village* (1832), typify that peculiarly humorous and nostalgic stance regarding the imagined threat to traditional rural moral constructs in the face of a modernity that removed a sense of place. Charles Lamb, for instance, had illustrated this contradistinction in his essay, "Mackery End, in Hertfordshire," in *Essays of Elia* (1823). In this, Lamb contrasts the city mentality with that of the country: "But the name of kindred and of cousinship was enough. Those slender ties, that prove slight as gossamer in the rending atmosphere of a metropolis, bind faster, as we found it, in hearty, homely, loving Hertfordshire."[2] Lamb's general image of domesticity, his capacity for conversation, indoor pursuits, and affection for living a circumscribed life were widely disseminated in the periodical press, and undoubtedly his personality came to signify a certain coziness and comfort in a world in which such commodities were becoming rare. This theme is sustained in *Our Village*, and then in *Cranford*. Gaskell extends the idea into such welcome Victorian concepts as self-help, communal cooperation, and family or neighborly morality. One foundation of Cranford society is willing work in a spirit of togetherness, as when a party is in preparation, and the narration device directly confronts the reader with the notion of center and periphery:

We were very busy too, one whole morning, before Miss Jenkins gave her party, in following her directions, and in cutting out and stitching together pieces of newspaper, so as to form little paths to every chair, set for the expected visitors, lest their shoes might dirty or defile the carpet. Do you make paper paths for every guest to walk upon in London?[3]

Of course, the interest in *Cranford* is not in an imagined region or province: it is simply the fascination with a moral fabric in decay. The attraction of a microcosm is that it can be easily traversed, and everyone knows your name. Strangers in the village are marked and noted, defined and judged in due course, and either accepted or rejected. Yet there is poverty here, just as Gaskell observed in Manchester. The difference is that this is "genteel" and therefore not a noted problem or even visible: "I imagine that a few of the gentlefolks of Cranford were poor, and had some difficulty in making ends meet; but they were like the Spartans, and concealed their smart under a smiling face."[4]

The insistence on "gentility" as an organizing principle of the ideology provides something that later in regional writing was to prove hard to shift: a precedent was available, inviting the writer to create a set of moral virtues in the notional center of the region. John Ridd in *Lorna Doone*, for instance, is given long and involved accounts of family bonds and regulations as the tale unfolds, and this in sharp contrast to that of, say, the Earnshaws of *Wuthering Heights*. Yet certainly the kernel of a loving community, held together by clear ideas of sustenance and communication, was asserted by Gaskell in her extension of Knutsford into fiction.

Arguably, this is an ideal point at which to juxtapose *regional* and *provincial*. In the earlier John Sutherland quote, the regional was interpreted as something predominantly imagined and invented; yet, with a broader definition, Peter Keating sees Victorian fiction rather differently. He makes the notion of realism the center here and then goes on:

Regional fiction was not only not dead, it was actually flourishing. The buoyant fiction market in books and periodicals offered unprecedented opportunities for "local" authors; and as the publishing industry became centred on London, it was easy to forget that there were active publishers in other English cities, and in Scotland, Wales and Ireland.[5]

When the notion of place is under threat, then the fears of uniformity initiate a fresh scrutiny of the particular. The fears about the namelessness of place were everywhere in the works of the Romantics: to name a place was part of the sacredness, the ritualistic celebration of its uniqueness. John Clare, for instance, celebrates in several poems the particularity of a place in terms of insisting on the power of difference in humanity. In "The Lamentations of Round-Oak Waters" he even personifies the place, creating a quasi-human lament, and in the process uses the classical idea of the genius loci:

> I am the genius of the brook
>   and like to thee I moan
> By Naiads and by all forsook
>   Unheeded and alone.[6]

The early Victorians had witnessed the coming of the railways and the process of enclosure; they had seen "place" transmute from settings for traditional pastimes to arenas of confrontation, such as Peterloo in 1819 or the Woodhouse moor of feasts and social life in Leeds witnessing the drilling of armed Chartists by Fergus O'Connor and his Physical Force Movement.

In this context, Cranford becomes redolent of small-scale values, recognizable parameters, and small horizons. It is no accident that Edwin Waugh's new proletariat in Lancashire were also contracting, scaling down to attainable boundaries in life:

> It's wise to be humble I'prosperous ways,
>   for trouble may chance to be nee;
> It's wise for to struggle wi' sorrowful days,
>   Till sorrow breeds sensible glee.[7]

The regional novel of invention extends this microcosmic known community into more adventurous areas of human experience. From one standpoint, this can be perceived in the changing perceptions of "the North" and its range of connotations. The geographical boundaries of north and south had been located in a variety of ways since the Middle Ages, but the Humber estuary across to the Mersey has been most generally accepted as the English (not British) boundary. This explains the sheer distance of Yorkshire from London in both literal and metaphorical terms. The terms Northerners and Yorkshiremen provide interesting information regarding the literary notions of regions in the early Victorian period.

Central to this is the history of the English novel and the point at which it had arrived by the time of Dickens in the late 1830s and when Gaskell's *North and South* made a deep impact on the North–South divide conceptions. In the social or industrial novels of the 1840s we have yet another cognate of truly regional writing, but this time the binary oppositions clustering around the Northern and Southern characters and places provide something more fundamental to constructs of the periphery. Raymond Williams talks about the "problems of the knowable community" and insists that this is a "matter of consciousness as well as of evident fact."[8] In *North and South* the whole idea of consciousness is dealt with in terms of a fundamental difference: the Northerner as a different mode of being, a bundle of manners and customs, attitudes and beliefs so removed from the Home Counties that Gaskell has to explain a confrontation as if she were a guide to an alien species. In *North and South* (1855) and in her *Life of Charlotte Brontë* (1857) she takes pains to introduce this other England within England in much the same way that twentieth-century documentarists revealed the submerged classes and their lifestyles. The fictional city of Milton-Northern is represented as a gigantic, threatening, and supernatural element with awesome power even before Margaret arrives in her journey from the south:

For several miles before they reached Milton, they saw a deep, lead-coloured cloud hanging over the horizon in the direction in which it lay. It was all the darker from contrast with the pale grey-blue of the wintry sky: for in Heston there had been the earliest signs of frost.[9]

It is a new kind of "region," almost created in the sense that Dante's *Inferno* envisioned regions of hell. The southern reader would have been prepared for the denizens of this place to be radically different from themselves, living under a man-made heaven—a people seemingly influencing the climate.

Thornton himself, although he longs for the attributes of a gentleman in his need for classical learning, is fundamentally perceived as a creature of his environment:

I should not like to bargain with him; he looks very inflexible. Altogether a man who seems made for his niche, mamma; sagacious and strong, as becomes a great tradesman.[10]

In other words, he is made to conform to a generally defined category within the definitions of the South: a "tradesman" in spite of his achievements. But Gaskell takes these representations further, and *North and South* becomes a regional *Ur-text* in the sense that it is not strictly a regional novel, but more a novel about social and professional difference. Thornton may have been molded by environment, but he exemplifies the central virtues of the Victorian ethos of self-help and discipline:

After a quiet life in a country parsonage for more than twenty years, there was something dazzling to Mr. Hale in the energy which conquered immense difficulties with ease; the power of the machinery in Milton, the power of the men in Milton, impressed him with a sense of grandeur.[11]

Gaskell was, of course, uniquely placed to see these surface differences, and she makes the environment a specific element with a creative but ambivalent potency: a notable example is the account of the mill girls when she writes about Crampton, around the mill. Here, the girls are part of a community without the female graces and deportment of southern gentility, yet they have a "rough, yet not unfriendly freedom."[12]

Work is the center of all this, of course, and Thornton's desire for a classical education is not understood generally, as it equates with the "idle" habits of university men. The effect of these oppositions in the novel is one of intended didacticism, and here the novel falls short of the true regional novel. Gaskell is stretching to overstate the physicality and robustness of a rising class in the new world of the entrepreneur and the proletariat. The novel charts the slippage of the "knowable community" often by means of the Romantic use of the countryside and the recent historical rural paradise depicted by Helstone. When Margaret speaks of Helstone to Bessy, it is linked with Bessy's dreams of Heaven:

I cannot tell you half its beauty. There are great trees standing all about it. . . . And then in other parts there are billowy ferns . . . some with great streaks of golden sunlight lying on them.[13]

This is a familiar dichotomy in Gaskell's fiction. The function of Alice in *Mary Barton* (1848) is similar: the rural past and the urban present are made to attain a higher level, to represent a lost world, a golden age, when the known community was certain and comforting. Cranford reaches the status of a visionary imagining in comparison to Manchester and Milton-Northern. Williams detects a radical reshifting of consciousness in the novels of this period; it comes as no surprise, then, to find Gaskell explaining a new phenomenon by means of the conventional subpastoral, which even found a place in Scott and the earlier picaresque. Rural England was becoming an invention well before its demise.

YORKSHIRE AS A PARADIGM

In her *Life of Charlotte Brontë* Gaskell produced a work of a very different tenor: here we have another version of explaining the distant alien being, one of her contemporaries, yet somehow frozen in time. She uses the first chapters of this book to explain her personal shock at being faced with a barren terrain and openly delivers a series of oral history anecdotes in order to confirm the readership of the Brontë novels in their view that Yorkshire people were more likely to be descendants of Shakespeare's rural clowns than actual people. That they were also definable in terms of occupation and class was also open to discussion, as she stresses their willful individuality in ways well beyond any norm of morality in the land, as in the story of the young man bleeding to death:

When my husband had checked the effusion of blood with a strap that one of the bystanders unbuckled from his leg, he asked if a surgeon had been sent for.
    "Yoi," was the answer, "But we dunna think ge'll come."
    "Why not?"
    "He's owd you see, and asthmatic, and it's up-hill."[14]

The second chapter is an extended account of these alien peoples, with statements about Yorkshiremen's hardness, love of profit, taciturnity, and combative sense of relationships. This clearly evinces the view that such fictional creations as Heathcliff and Hareton Earnshaw may indeed be found in the moors and dales of the area.

It is useful to reflect at this point on why Yorkshire should be so fascinating to the Victorians. The evidence points to the fact that it was an area waiting to be put on the literary map. Emily Brontë obviously extended her imaginings of the inhabitants of her childhood world of Gondal into her Yorkshiremen, and *Wuthering Heights* effectively juxtaposes the mythic Heathcliff (not too far from the youthful Julius Brenzaida of Gondal) with such preaching, life-denying souls as Joseph. But the fictional effects of these mixtures are deepened when we consider the dialect.

In depicting Joseph as the typical bible-thumping moralist inhabiting the loft in the Heights, Emily Brontë chose to give him to her readers through the relentlessly baffling medium of dialect, and research has shown that her dialect is very accurately given phonetically for the location of Howarth near the Yorkshire–Lancashire border. But Joseph's language is brilliantly powerful in the context of Lockwood's (and all readers') sense of confrontation with a different scale of being:

Aw woonder hagh yah can faishon tuh stand theear l'idleness un war, when all on 'em's goan aght! Bud yah're a nowt and it's noah use talkin'.[15]

It is easy to see the literary forebears in Scott's characters with their chorus-like humors and their functions as local color, but Joseph is so meticulously included as a version of the famous local preacher, Parson Grimshaw. But the question is, how did Emily's personal vision of all-consuming love ascend, along with the story of *Jane Eyre*, into a massive mythic version of "Yorkshire," depicting supposedly quintessentially "Northern" qualities? Lucasta Miller's book, *The Brontë Myth,* sets out to explain the sources of the various Brontë myths that have been developed over the years, as writers and critics have distorted the facts—a process that began early on, with William Dearden's reporting of Branwell Brontë's claim to have written much of *Wuthering Heights.* But Miller's main concern is (rightly) the "cult of Emily" and the notion of the "mystic of the moors." Even this geographical foundation of the novel has been taken largely as an aspect of "mysticism" rather than a Yorkshire setting—that is, the moors need not be in Yorkshire, but simply a place of a particular vision.

As Miller relates, even the place is in some ways derivative, relating to certain elements in Scott's *The Black Dwarf*: "Like Lockwood, . . . Earncliff [in Scott's novel] finds himself holed up in a solitary moorland dwelling with the eponymous dwarf, a piteous but horrifying character, who has, like Heathcliff, turned misanthrope."[16] Therefore, the interest in the myth of the Brontës has been often more that supposed mystical Romanticism than the Yorkshire of the setting. But a remark of John Hewish, in his study of Emily Brontë, has perhaps not been taken up with the thoroughness and curiosity it deserves. Hewish is commenting on Scott's influence: "This is another instance of writers in whom he awoke a new sense of region."[17]

We should ask what this sense was. Criticism of *Wuthering Heights* has included such inquiry, but the Yorkshire that Emily creates was at the time so distant from London, so unknown (even with the new railways in mind), that the historical origins of the communal fabric of the Dales and the Lancashire border have to be acknowledged in the novel as something conceived as "wild" and unmannered. Clearly, the oppositional force of Earnshaws and Lockwoods makes some textual realizations of Northern character accessible. In broad terms, it is given in terms of "civilized" values against the untutored, the uneducated. When the dogs are set on Heathcliff and Cathy outside Thrushcross Grange, the impact is one of Yorkshire as an alien threat, a barbarian assault on the domesticity and family stability of the inner world of Thrushcross. Cathy and Heathcliff may be spiritually united and in some kind of instinctual life of the spirit on the moors, but they are also a strand of the Victorian binary opposition of the civilized and the barbarian. Emily Brontë reminded southern readers that Victorian society contained some exclusions: the regional invention she makes is one in which the weather becomes a dominating metaphor for the un-contained, the emotive factor of subversion found in the streets of the new towns and in the inclemency of certain moral values of the periphery of consciousness. The place itself is described in this way:

Wuthering Heights is the name of Mr. Heathcliff's dwelling. "Wuthering" being a significant provincial adjective, descriptive of the atmospheric tumult to which its station is exposed in stormy weather. Pure bracing ventilation they must have up there.[18]

The passage goes on to extend a metaphorical counterpart to the people themselves, using an account of "gaunt thorns all stretching their limbs one way, as if craving alms of the sun."[19] The prevalence in the novel of walls and windows, light and dark is often related to the Earnshaws themselves, and it is clear that Emily Brontë was explaining this rough Northern breed in the realms of natural phenomena, instinctive beings living outside the pale.

After all, Yorkshire in the eighteenth century had meant crime, a bolt-hole of the underclass. It was where Dick Turpin hailed from, and the Halifax Coiners had hidden from the forces of law in the narrow heights of Heptonstall, over the moors from Howarth. Returning to Elizabeth

Gaskell's explanation of Yorkshire people and customs, it is interesting to note the prominence given to the aggressive and tough nature of the hill people: "still there are remaining of this class—dwellers in the lonely houses far away in the upland districts" with a "wild strength of will."[20] That is, Yorkshire contains that enigma: a tribe without a sense of community; a people for whom the concept of civilized values is beyond recognition. The Victorian media representations of popular communal belonging were a crusade to create unity or consensus in a land of disparate histories and identities.

In the context of the political history of the Romantic period, notions of Yorkshire were no different from prevailing concepts of Ireland or Scotland or Wales. The common history of all these places had been borderlands. The Pale in Ireland, the Highlands in Scotland and the West of Wales, and the Lleyn—all were distant places in which civilized values did not apply, and hence the regional writers had something to explain. Scott's repeated juxtapositions of Anglicized and "wild" Scots typify this, and Emily Brontë learned from him the attraction of wild, unknown lands for Romantic literature. Whereas Wales or the Lakes had become places of grand aesthetic conceptions such as "sublime" or "picturesque," Yorkshire had been one of the forgotten regions, still an unmeasured, featureless border, as it had been in the Tudor period—a place that had to be fortified along the river valleys in the northern Dales when the Scropes and the Ricardians had taken control. But it has to be recalled that in the Jacobite rebellions Yorkshire and Lancashire men had rallied to the call of the Scots, and the power of the Northumberland aristocracy was still a feature of life.

For all these reasons, *Wuthering Heights* and Gaskell's *Life of Charlotte Brontë* are arguably best judged as some of the very first regional texts to account for this great unknown tract of land that had only recently become prominent on the economic map with the acceleration of technology in the woolen industry and the new importance of the Pennine streams and mills.

IRELAND AND NEW REPRESENTATIONS

In his study of Irish cultural history, *The Irish Story*, R. F. Foster is concerned with how contemporary Ireland has become a notable paradigm for the theme-park cultural heritage trend. This is so, even to the extent of a theme park dedicated to the Great Famine having been organized in West Limerick. England has been given an invention of Ireland so egregiously distorted and unthinking that, in terms of literary history, the huge presence of the Famine at the heart of the decade now under discussion is problematical when trying to understand how the "region" of Ireland was textualized at the time.

In an interview, Foster commented that "In Ikea they tell you how to shop. It's a path you have to follow and you can't deviate from it. . . . Theme park history works the same way, assuming that history is a story with a beginning, middle and an end."[21] The case is that in nineteenth-century England, Ireland and the Irish were conceived of in very narrow, entrenched ways. In his essay on "Irish Literature and Irish History," Declan Kiberd has provided a very perceptive analysis of the situation regarding the representation of Ireland in this context. For the present study, his account of the novel is particularly useful. He surveys the Irish novel from Maria Edgeworth's *Castle Rackrent* (1800) to the strikingly realistic fiction of William Carleton, and he notes: "So charged did the situation become that Maria Edgeworth abandoned her career as an Irish novelist, writing to her brother in 1834: 'It is impossible to draw Ireland as she is now in a book of fiction—realities are too strong—party passions are too violent to bear or see.'"[22]

With this in mind, it is startling to note the persistence of caricatured Irish people and customs in the popular novels of such writers as Samuel Lover and Charles Lever, whose works were populated by, as Kiberd says, "feckless, good-natured bumpkins who struck a happy-go-lucky pose in the midst of poverty and ill fortune."[23]

In a preface to his novel, *Handy Andy*, in 1842, Lover felt it necessary to write an apologia for his penchant for melodrama and slight but stereotyped comedy: "I have been accused of giving flattering portraits of my countrymen," and he continues that, like a painter, he has the habit of "taking the best view of my subject, so long prevalent in my eye."[24] This is an ingenuous and potentially offensive defense of an aesthetic that merely refuses to think about the surface comedy of his fiction—a mode that unashamedly exploits racial and cultural stereotypes. In *Handy Andy*, for instance, the eponymous protagonist causes all kinds of anger, confusion, and personal danger to others, yet it is all supposed to be a narrative of forgivable, harmless bungling in a person whose people are there to adorn life with entertainment, not to truly think or act with dignity.

Ireland, then, as a "region" if not a "nation," was a crucially important literary subject in the 1840s, and it needed a writer to see that it was given rather than betrayed to English readers. A reading of the Irish fiction of that decade initiates a great deal of productive thought about the Victorian conception of the "Celtic peoples" who were to form part of Matthew Arnold's conceptions of high culture a little later in the century. The Celtic Twilight of the 1890s contains some elements of distortion and myth, but the imaginings and patterns of belonging seen in Carleton are an acute and enlightening version of more profound and complex aspects of Irish identity than are ever even hinted at in the representations of the Samuel Lover/stage-Irishman traditions.

William Carleton's fiction is remarkable for many reasons. The title of his most successful works, *Traits and Stories of the Irish Peasantry* (definitive edition 1842–1844), implies the paradox of being somehow related to oral narrative and yet fixed in a rather pejorative terminology for the 1840s—"peasantry"—a word indicative of both folk beyond real consideration in the metropolis, but which had been given a new dignity in titles of works such as John Clare, Robert Bloomfield, and their subgenre. Carleton was something of a wandering scholar, educated at a hedge school,[25] and a man who had been actively involved in sectarian violence, traveled for work, and converted from Catholic to Protestant. He discovered his vocation as a writer and obviously realized the immense potential for writing with real authenticity about his own people.

But regional writing or national writing, depending on the viewpoint, involves a necessary infusion of the didactic, as the writer has to explain and define something to strangers. As Declan Kiberd comments: "To Carleton's ear Irish eloquence in English was suspect, a sign of a people who might congratulate themselves on being fluent without ever really becoming articulate. The baroque language of hedge-schoolmasters might gull credulous parents. . . . But it was hardly a vehicle for the pressure of real feeling."[26] This conflict is evident in Carleton's style. He is bookish, imbued with the elegance and symmetry of Augustan prose, as if his writing is modeled on the Johnsonian essays and *belles lettres* of a previous age. His learning is sometimes a burden, and he needs copious footnotes. Yet there is still a genuine sense of lived experience in his stories. This emanates from the oral feel, the tone of the easy raconteur by the fireside, despite the learning of the purposeful collector of rural tales. Beneath the popular racy manner, there is a profound comprehension of the dynamics of Irish society and the specific notion of community in the culture and literature.

To a modern reader, Carleton's stories exhibit the same tendency as Scott's novels in the process of uncovering a lost way of life: they have to demonstrate thought and action so remote that the argot of expression and the intonations of their speech present a sense of artifice. This artifice springs from a creative mix of affection and a desire for truth. In his introduction to the stories, Carleton makes the basis of his art clear: "It is well known that the character of the Irishman has been hitherto uniformly associated with something unusually ridiculous."[27] From this, he moves on to compare the two nations of England and Ireland at that time, and he stresses that in the previous age Ireland had been "incapable of presenting anything to the world but a school book or a pamphlet."[28] The introduction is full of the confidence of a writer whose recounted life is clearly one of a witness as well as of a participant; he resolves to speak of life in Ireland—its "loves, sorrows, superstitions, pieties, amusements, crimes and virtues"—and he says "with solemn truth" that he has told the story honestly.[29]

A summary of the methods used in his narratives sheds light on how regional writers—those explaining the periphery to the center—tend to work when they have to fuse explanation with fictional modes. A typical example is *The Lough Derg Pilgrim*, as it uses autobiography, discursive style, and anecdotal narrative. This piece is of special interest because, as Kiberd comments: "For Carleton, the pilgrimage to Station Island revealed not only the impossibility of a vocation to the Catholic priesthood but also the urgency of his vocation to writing."[30] The piece is essentially an account of the whole ritual, a predesigned circuit of pilgrimage; but added to this is another level of narrative, which deals with the strictly contemporary Ireland and embraces both the more anecdotal story of a theft but also a slight but telling reference to the year—and the famine. He says almost simply in passing: "It is right to mention here that this pilgrimage was performed in a season when sickness and famine prevailed fearfully in this kingdom."[31]

Then follows a scene in which a father with his sick son tries to avoid paying the priest. The son is wretchedly ill and hungry, and Carleton juxtaposes the two modes of didactic anecdote and genuinely powerful realism. The two do not sit entirely successfully together, but the point is that any hint of the maudlin or sentimental is avoided. What it does have is a potent commentary on the institutionalism of the Catholic Church, and the tough morality of the believer under such duress.

Yet Carleton can also provide a different mix of folk raconteur and social commentary, as in "The Hedge School," a lengthy piece of fiction comprising almost an essay-style account of the nature of the hedge school with a tale of abduction equal to any adventure in *Don Quixote*. Carleton, in depicting Ireland through his unique fusion of realism and scholarly Augustan style, creates a new vision of the land. Seen as a "region" from London or even Dublin, his rural Ireland is given as a fascinating balance of brutality, suffering, and enlightened lust for learning.

Traits and Stories of the Irish Peasantry furnishes something of an interim text, between the arrival of the Irish Renaissance at the turn of the century and the earlier caricatures of Samuel Lover, whose style is more that of the sporty blade at the fireside in the inn, relating tales of high jinks and foolishness. It has to be said that Lover was responsible for perpetuating representations of Ireland that dwelt on the Romanticism, as in his account of a character called Edward O'Connor in *Handy Andy:*

It was shrewdly suspected he was a poet; it was less well known he was highly educated and accomplished; and yet Edward O'Connor was a universal favourite, bore the character of being "a real fine fellow" and was loved and respected by the most illiterate of the young men; who, in allusion to his extensive lore on the *romantic* history of Ireland, his own Christian name, and his immediate place of residence, which was near a wild mountain pass, christened him "Ned of the Hill."[32]

Carleton, in taking his subject more seriously, delivered a view of Ireland that made a prominent place for its learning and instinctive sense of art and creativity—the Ireland, for instance, that the young Patrick Bronte left, to go from a hedge school to be a sizar at St. John's College, Cambridge.

GEORGE BORROW AND VICTORIAN WALES

Also within this twenty-year transitional period, when the Celtic nations were still regions to visit on artistic grand tours in order to experience the "picturesque," Wales saw a radical shift in self-awareness, and traditions were invented that were to have a bearing on Anglo–Welsh writing forty years after George Borrow's account of the country in 1862. Throughout the previous century, before Borrow, the cultural and literary life of Wales had been mostly perceived from England as a matter of druids, mountains, and bards. Mainly through the poetry of Thomas Gray, whose poem "The Bard" had had a considerable impact on constructions of Romantic Wales, and then Wordsworth at Tintern Abbey, the subject had been rather one-dimensional.

Then, as Prys Morgan has outlined in an admirable essay on inventing Wales,[33] between 1815 (the date of the new *eisteddfodau*—festivals of competition for prizes in literature, music, and drama) and 1847 (the year of the Blue Books on Wales), there was a transformation. This was largely due to Iolo Morganwg (real name, Edward Williams), who did a great deal to promote such notions as druids, the Gorsedd of Bards, promotional insignia, and general ritualistic conceptions that would appeal to those who wanted to construct the idea of Wales from a mix of the Romantic and the mock-medieval. At times this meant using formerly quite obscure historical events and personages as fresh symbols of Welshness. The literature emanating from this movement, at least in English, was of minimal importance, but the period saw the social and institutional elements of Welsh identity very much settled and confirmed.

Morganwg was "a wild dreamer, a lifelong addict to laudanum, a drug which caused hallucinations . . . was driven by historical myths and in turn he used historical myths to create new traditions which had profound, far-reaching effects."[34] These effects, though mainly in terms of cultural trends, did find a resonance after the Blue Books: a Royal Commission into the state of Wales that blamed the Welsh language for the dissent and backwardness of the Welsh people (so called because it was bound in blue books). After 1847, there was more evidence of political militancy. An intellectual and aesthetic dichotomy appeared, primarily concerning those who looked back to preindustrial Wales for the simple nonconformist culture and those who saw political and commercial developments as being formative of a new consciousness.

The interesting aspect of all this is that there was no real Anglo–Welsh literature at this time. In his survey of nineteenth-century writing in this category, Roland Mathias can only include notably peripheral writing in English on Wales, such as that of Thomas Love Peacock, R. D. Blackmore, and Charles Kingsley, but these are only Welsh settings. Thomas Pritchard's *The Adventures and Vagaries of Twm Sion Catti* (1828), he notes, "has some claim to be called the first novel in English from Wales," but is marked by what Mathias calls "flummery."[35] What he calls the "first flowering" of Anglo–Welsh writing does not arrive until the last twenty years of the century.

These aspects of Wales and Welsh writing apart, it is arguably George Borrow's *Wild Wales* (1862) that most initiated an English interest in the region beyond Offa's Dyke and in fact opened up some of the deeper and more complex aspects of Welsh identity to discussion. Outstanding in Borrow's inquiry as he travels the land on foot is the extent to which ordinary Welsh people are truly affirmative of the supposed mythic "land of song" and of the Bards. Lady Charlotte Guest had published her famous edition of the Welsh tales of the *Mabinogion* in 1849; in 1856 the now famous national anthem, "Land of My Fathers," was written and published by Evan and James James of Pontypridd; also, Augusta Waddington had created the typical Welsh female attire we now associate with Wales in its heritage identity. Prys Morgan writes: "Within a very short time she and her friends had evolved a homogenized national costume from . . . various Welsh peasant dresses."[36]

George Borrow, then, was wandering in a place newly promoted as a land of bards and singers, with a deep and rather esoteric culture; in fact, he expected to find a land in which people of all classes would be steeped in Welsh literature and lore. The book is mostly concerned with North Wales and so deals with the rural Wales of the Romantic vision. Borrow also finds what he is looking for, constantly elevating talk of poets into areas of immense literary significance by combining ideas of locality, reputation, and sheer mystique. Typical of this is his encounter with a woman near Llangollen with whom he discusses first Iolo Goch, the "bard of Glyndwr," and then Thomas Edwards (Twm o'r Nant, who had died in 1810). Borrow was astounded that the woman knew nothing of Iolo Goch and yet knew of Edwards. The reply he gives the woman explains much of Borrow's affection for "greatness" and the more high-culture elements in Welsh literary history, which he loved to set against a pattern of poetry in the mouths of ordinary folk—a theme running through the whole book: "The reason is that the poet whom you mentioned, wrote in the old measures and language which few people understand, whilst Thomas Edwards wrote in common verse and in the language of the present day."[37]

Borrow was determined to find a Welsh literary folk culture set against the bookish and learned image of the newly fostered Gorsedd and *eisteddfodau*; he was undoubtedly well schooled in Gray's "The Bard," a poem set at the time of Edward I, when all the bards of Wales were ordered to be killed. This prophetic poem contains the lines: "The verse adorn again / Fierce War and faithful Love / and truth severe. By fairy fiction drest."[38] This line of thought surely existed in Borrow's attitude—that is, that Wales was, in contrast to England, a place in which some pure strain of classic poetry, rhetorical and noble, was evidenced in a cultured and cultivated people. After all, he had studied the Celtic languages for literary purposes and as a traveler reveled in mixing the bookish with the hearty and manful, as when he joined a field of land-workers and was taught how to use a scythe.

Borrow likes to display his mastery of Welsh and to initiate those playful paradoxes in which languages upset the norms, present challenges to orthodoxy, as in several people's amazement that an Englishman would want to learn Welsh. In the context of the recent Blue Books, his venture into being a Welsh speaker would have been all the more subversive and amazing to the lower classes in Wales in particular. *Wild Wales* is a rare example of a book that asserts a vision of a region almost by accident. The overt reason for writing the book is no more than curiosity—first aroused by the language that gave the world the man whom Borrow considered the greatest lyric poet of Europe, Dafydd ap Gwilym—but also the fascination communicated by the Welsh groom from whom he learned some Welsh before the journey. In a sense it is a book in the genre of the literary quest, as if he were Boswell to Wales, an interpreter of an alien place for those who only know the "Taffy was a Welshman" rhyme and perhaps Shakespeare's Fluellen.

Yet Borrow succeeds in generating a vision of a Wales beyond the realities of what was in his time a growing industrial nation. The red skies of the south of Wales are anathema; he wishes to extend the medieval image of Wales, the country of the bards and their patrons, and yet raise rural Wales from a place of simple toil to a true "Gwlad Beirdd"—land of poets—as in the national anthem.

In trying to create a version of the linguist's heaven or a country teeming with songsters, Borrow succeeds in reversing the inquiry, and attention is drawn to himself more than to his subjects. Repeatedly, his comments gather to indicate a will to make a Wales of the mind. For instance, he judges Wrexham on grounds that simply define Borrow himself as the outsider who feels that he knows Wales in some way because he knows the language. He builds his opinion on etymology: that Wrexham is a Saxon compound with Wroxham (in his own Norfolk), and he notes that the people do not have the "look" of Welshmen. In this thinking he is imbued with the mid-Victorian imperial ideology of Celt and Saxon, as in *Hereward the Wake*, Kingsley's historical novel of 1866 in which the myth of the Saxon as a Victorian male prototype is propounded.

The linguistic imperial sway of English is never questioned by Borrow, and he is always in danger of treating the other languages he learned as curiosities. It is possible to construct a topography of "Wales" in Borrow that is essentially a mental landscape—one in which language defines certain deeper qualities of character and aligns with racial features. This leads him to make wild generalizations about his "wild" Wales.

The interest of the 1840–1860 period for regional writing, then, is that it saw the formation of a series of templates that would come to house the flowering of regional writing and the versions of literary belonging so prominent in the last decades of the century. The massive social and demographic change of the first half of the century meant that a new and more purposeful type of regional belonging would have room to progress: town and country became equally important in this context, but the myth of England was always at the center, and it will be necessary to examine the Wessex of Thomas Hardy and the Potteries of Arnold Bennett not only with the new cities in mind, but also countermovements such as the English folk song revival and the literary regionalism of the Kailyard.

Between 1860 and 1880, the notions of "region" and "province" drift apart in their range of social connotations. George Eliot's work remains provincial, as she is more concerned with social networks and the struggle for individual identity than with imagining a place or a place in the mind; and the true archetype of the literary region appears with *Lorna Doone*.

Yet within these twenty years surveyed above, there emerged a set of regional mental imaginings, based on projected and distorted history and literary history of mythic proportions. Scotland's Highlands reached a pinnacle of myth as Landseer painted them and Queen Victoria stayed there; Scotland became "the Highlands" much in the same way as Ruritania was to become a vaguely bohemian place somewhere east of Vienna; Wales was struggling to be seen as more than tall hats and druids in long coats; but, thanks to Carleton, Ireland was to be realized and delivered as much more than something perceived with laughter against stereotypes.

3

Countries of the Mind:
From Wessex to the Kailyard

Between Hardy's first truly Wessex novel, *Far from the Madding Crowd* (1874), and J. M. Barrie's *Margaret Ogilvy by Her Son* (1897), regional writing came of age. In those twenty-three years remarkable advances were made in the invention of regions as more than rural idylls. They became a statement of a counterculture, often crossing boundaries with the neopastoral and rural realism of such writers as Richard Jefferies. But also in those decades, Arnold Bennett made his Five Towns arguably the first template for social naturalism in the depiction of regional consciousness. Hardy and Bennett form a fascinating oppositional counterpoint, going deeper than country–city contrasts; they both suggest the complexity of modernity within the center of culture and the new modes of being in the post–Industrial Revolution revisions of man.

Also, the Scottish novelists of the Kailyard and their influence provide one of the best-documented case studies of regional belonging in British fiction. They raise fresh issues about the vernacular and the place of local dialect in writing, and they provide certain questions about the nature of sentimentality—an unstable concept in most cases but seen as such *in extremis* in the case of Crockett, for instance. Dialect is common to all these works; Hardy in particular was troubled by this representation from the start of his career, but when his work was edited by Edmund Gosse, the narrative was sharpened and made more suitable for the new readership of the commuter class and the newly enlarged middle classes.

Dialect and dialogue could be offered as the central problematic factor of regional writing. The locals have to be given "as they are," but the existing connotations of the regional in the minds of metropolitan editors, publishers, and readers are another thing altogether, being formed by media representations perhaps poorly conceived and wildly inaccurate. When Hardy first emerged as a writer, his dialogue was given easily and fluently phonetically, with a fondness for creating situations in which the reader experiences the local talk through channels of uncertainty. This had the effect of making the talk a set piece and often a transparent plot-device, as in the scene in *Far from the Madding Crowd* when Gabriel is hidden on the back of the wagon as the farmworkers talk in front:

"Be as 'twill, she's a fine handsome body as far's looks be concerned. But that's only the skin of the woman, and these dandy cattle be as proud as a lucifer in their insides."
"Aye—so's a do seem, Billy Smallbury—so'a do seem."
"She's a very vain feymell—so 'tis said her and there."[1]

It is clear from this that Hardy was using his novelist's ear for talk and integrating the product using simple techniques, such as giving a character's name in the dialogue. But the extensive use of country characters and dialogue in *Under the Greenwood Tree* (1872), his overtly pastoral novel, obviously placed him in readers' minds as someone who used the choral and comic contrast possibilities of "yokels" as a kind of Mummerset. Hence the consequent difficulties when *The Return of the Native* was reviewed in *The Athenaeum* in 1878. Raymond Chapman has written on the issue of speech representation as criticized in the journal, and he has pinpointed Hardy's troubles on this score.[2] The main complaint was the use of a language that would establish "the grotesque element." In fact, the notion of authentic representation of speech becomes one of the most contentious aspects of regional texts in the modern period, and Chapman's discussion is useful for understanding the negative criticisms put against the Kailyard, and even against John Synge in later writing.

As Chapman says, the problem was that Hardy was accused of making his peasants "too refined and sophisticated in their speech," but the point is also one of naturalistic representation and how readers from the cultural centers are supposed to find and use criteria for properly understanding the use of dialect in writing. Hardy's preface to the 1912 edition of *The Mayor of Casterbridge* is enlightening here, because he faces up to criticisms concerning the Scottish character, Farfrae. Hardy's defense is: "It must be remembered that the Scotchman of the tale is represented not as he would appear to other Scotchmen, but as he would appear to people of outer regions. Moreover, no attempt is made to reproduce his entire pronunciation phonetically, any more than that of the Wessex speakers."[3] Chapman's long discussion concludes that Hardy's use of dialect "sets him above most of his fellows, handling the unfamiliar variations with regard to character and situation."[4]

This question of authentic speech as opposed to dialogue that makes concessions to the readership and to generic convention is a major part of the regional literature of Britain, being fundamental to the intentions of the writer. Whether the aim is to simply reflect people and attitudes or to insert a particular didactic element in the writing, the result is always one with a specific problem: intelligibility. In Hardy's case, Wessex is at stake, as the reader's acceptance of the idea of Wessex depends on the delivery of that particular quality of narrative that Hardy conceived.

There is little point in explaining the nature of Hardy's Wessex here; it has been done admirably by several writers. But the immediate context in this chapter is to place Wessex in the literary historical frame of regional constructs, and in that paradigm it is one of the most sustained and comprehensive regional inventions in the whole of our literature. Hardy's Wessex is defined by a particular quality of theatricality. His narratives often very purposefully bring modernity and traditional, cyclical rural life into conflict, but the real narrative interest is always one of the imprint of place and belonging on the individual. Of course, some of his protagonists are archetypal Victorian souls in unrest and aspiring for their place in the amelioration of man in the "enlightened" age of Darwin and new science, but they are also compounds of home and community at odds with their inner desires. "Region" for Hardy is a place located at the emotive center of being, constructed by a myriad factors, some found in family ties and others in acquired learning, but all equally formative.

One of the paradoxes of Hardy's fiction is that the stage is often very suggestive of the artifice of narrative technique: readers feel the sense of the chessmen being moved, or the design being framed with an openly observable intention. When this is related to what he wants to say about local belonging and the sense of place, the result is often a symbolic encounter. In *Far from the Madding Crowd* we have the basic template for this—a method of writing that became massively influential on later regional writers—for instance, when Gabrial Oak saves the hay-ricks from fire damage:

Round the corner of the largest stack, out of the direct rays of the fire, stood a pony, bearing a young woman on its back . . .
    "He's a shepherd," said the woman on foot. "Yes he is. See how his crook shines as he beats the rick with it. And his smock-coat is burnt in two holes, I declare! A fine young shepherd he is too, ma'am."[5]

The fire and his attire become a separate world from the women and the horses; Oak has materialized from the night, brought there by destiny, to reclaim the life of the women he loves. Hardy sets this in a language of local fixedness—the smock, the hay-rick, the crook, all reinforce the elemental oneness of Oak with the work of the land, distinct from the new business world, now owned by a woman. It is as if Hardy wants to insist that character emanates from place, shaped by the particularity of words and things. Words and things become dominant: people are made and defined by their work, their simple possessions. The impulse of regional belonging thus appropriates the generic qualities of narrative poetry. Not only are Hardy's people an integral part of Wessex, they are instruments of its survival and sustenance. The force of love and attachment and even the romantic urge to devotion seem held within a larger mechanism of place and organic togetherness.

Hardy's early life and relatives gave him the source material, of course. He used the experiences and characters of his mother and certain uncles in the early books, and, as Robert Gittings has shown, the suicide of his friend, Horace Moule, in Cambridge also gave him one of his elements of the modern ailment of *Angst,* permeating several books and perhaps being the basis of Boldwood in *Far from the Madding Crowd.*[6]

One of the most enlightening contrastive studies to be made on Hardy's fiction is to put *Under the Greenwood Tree* by the side of *Far from the Madding Crowd*, because the shift from delicate, light pastoral to tragic narrative highlights the radical one toward depicting a regional consciousness of a real substance as opposed to an idyllic one that is more at home with Mary Russell Mitford and Elizabeth Gaskell than with Wessex. Again, Raymond Chapman's essay pinpoints the nature of the earlier novel: he talks about the collective function of the crowd, its choric nature, and its usefulness in making the rural set-piece scenes such as marriage or a concert more set in a timeless vision of that England of Shakespeare's history plays and comedies. Chapman points out that Hardy's language also includes idiophonic conversation—that is, he uses very particular individual traits of speech to differentiate people, as in the character of Smallbury in *Far from the Madding Crowd*, where he uses hesitancy and stuttering to add some light comedy.[7]

This topic of authentic speech is at the core of regional writing: arguably, the primary function of a regional text is to celebrate difference by means of overcoming the habitualization of the locally familiar and to expand this into a vision by defamiliarizing. In this way, regional writing is similar to children's writing in that it has to revise the processes of thought by which we lose the sharpness of interest in what is too close to us. In regional belonging and its literary visions, often symbolically expressed, we have the thesis that in the British sense of place there is a need to locate community through familiar ritual, divorced from actual ideological meanings. Thus Hardy's Wessex is an arena for the dynamics of the familiar social functions to be heightened into a dramatic role akin to classical Greek drama. He places mystery at the heart of the narrative devices and complicates the familiar so that, by circumstance and chance, it becomes almost malevolent. In Eustacia Vye, for instance, her external presence on the fringe of the society, seen as "odd" and as having special powers of mind, only serves to provide an insight into the habits of thought of the normal figures.

Like Clare, Hardy set about to represent the rural as a site of specifically paradoxical experience in relation to modernity. Where he uses a methodical and deliberate symbolism in *Tess of the D'Urbervilles*, for instance, in which modernity means haste, speed, engines, and regulated education, the opposite force is a version of blissful ignorance. The latter would seem to lead Tess's parents into destitution, but they never feel, as she does, the "ache of modernity," nor do they attain the potential of being tragic protagonists. But that modernity was also, with social history in mind, an ideology of empire and sexism too, and Angel Clare's need to "find himself" in South America is entirely in keeping with that late-Victorian mind-set of maleness and empire.

In contrast, the region of Wessex becomes a process of opposition to assert the eternal human values of community. While Hardy was writing his tragic novels, social trends moving toward the creation of mythic, invented traditions involving the rural communities were accelerating. As Georgina Boyes has shown, the "folk" of the Folk Song Society was an entirely artificial concept, a willed creation composed of nostalgia and Arcadia: "Whilst not deployed on the same occasions, the symbolic power of contemporary national pageantry was effectively reinforced by the prior existence of communal exhibition customs such as Morris dancing, well dressings and wakes processions."[8]

As Hardy was providing an antimodern diatribe in his narratives of Tess and Jude, the English Folk Song Society and the rituals of the new industrial towns with their civic ceremonies were celebrating regional identity through a reclamation of what we now call "heritage culture." This severely influences our modern view of regional belonging in this period.

LORNA DOONE

R. D. Blackmore's *Lorna Doone* (1869) is arguably the most quintessentially regional novel in English. Simon Trezise, in his magisterial study of "the West Country" in literature, has explained that the novel is rich in a basis of oral history and tradition as much as in a literary artifice made by a bookish scholarly writer. It represents the fundamental "West Country" of the imagination, and Trezise finds the origins of this construct in a similar domain to that of the Celt: "The Victorian Celt is very likely to be associated with all those pejorative terms linked with the rural: he is often 'savage' and 'barbaric.' While an English peasant is liable to be ignorant, a Celtic one is liable to be both ignorant and violent."[9] One does not have to look far in the novel to see this "barbarism"—the murder of Jan's father early in the story is evidence enough.

The essential core of the narrative as a regional tale is the fastness of the Doones' valley—their life and identity beyond the railways and far from the main routes. The timeless metaphors of roads and highways, settled communities and those beyond the pale, all reach out into metaphor in this many-layered novel. When Jan rides with Uncle Ben and they see the Doone home in the distance, the Uncle immediately thinks of destroying it, referring to his military experience:

Three culverins on yonder hill, and three on the top of this one—and we have them under a pestle. Ah, I have seen the wars my lad, from Keinton up to Naseby; and I might have been a general now if they had taken my advice.[10]

The novel is constantly violent, where people live on the edge of uncertainty. It begins with a fight, a test of strength, and it soon becomes, among other things, a story of difference maintained by tough aggression. Trezise summarizes the emergence of the Doone story in the hands of other writers and points out the variety of treatments of the theme in a range of Sedgemoor stories and Doone banditry tales. He then defines the source of Blackmore's art in making the story his own: "this word-picture images the landscape of memory and romance, the internal world coexisting with the outer world, the place of 'dark waters' encountered by Jan Ridd as he grows to manhood."[11]

Throughout the novel, we have a sense of the structures of family communal morality and behavior: a labyrinth of allegiances, duties, opinions, and protocols as strong as anything in Heathcliff's domain. Ridd's family itself, and the wider connections paying visits and helping in the broader education of the young man, are all *exempla* of the nature of oral history and myth. Blackmore unashamedly includes long didactic sections, long-winded digressions in speech, and convoluted explanations of lore and belief. Yet these seem naturally organic to the narrative's main devices and the overall storyline.

The most profoundly regional elements, however, are the romantic and emotional fusions of rugged places and powerful feelings. Blackmore does what Hardy also likes to do: relate place to inner fears or yearnings. Climbing to the Doone homeland, Ridd confesses: "The look of the place had a sad effect, scaring me very greatly, and making me feel that I would give something, only to be at home again, with Annie cooking my supper."[12]

This is entirely typical of the regional stance on the sheer adventure of place: an assertion of the basic, very English binary opposition of home and alien, stability and the unknown. *Lorna Doone* has the unmistakable quality of making what should be a familiar and defined region of Britain very much a threatening, foreign place, as distant from the central cultural media constructions as the Yorkshire moors or the Scottish borders. Blackmore was certainly one of the writers who gave British literature its sense of place and history intermixing to play a part in the destinies of modern people, caught up in the roots of the past and the accelerated change of the modern age.

BENNETT AND THE FIVE TOWNS

With the work of Arnold Bennett we begin to consider that aspect of regional writing in which the literary invention is created and sustained from a point of distance or even exile. Bennett's Five Towns were forged into a mythic region by him, once his literary ambitions were being fulfilled in London and elsewhere. He had the task of turning a very unattractive area of spoilheaps and potteries into a human place where people formed relationships and discovered their inner sense of identity despite the formidably puritan and life-denying utilitarianism of their environment. This theme of self-knowledge against the odds in an unfeeling world became a formative narrative for the later Northern and Midlands writers of the 1950s, but Bennett was breaking new ground. In relation to Gaskell's fiction of Manchester, for instance, Bennett creates characters and themes from within, from his inner experience among the production; Gaskell is always the visitor, for all her empathic abilities as a writer.

As Margaret Drabble has pointed out, Bennett found the capability to write about the Five Towns with a certain affection and a heightening of their nature: something he learned from George Moore. Drabble quotes Bennett's journal entry for 10 December 1897 to note that Bennett was able to appreciate the homeland as something special for him and something with the potential to be lifted into an invented fiction for a regional assertion of difference:

Down below is Burslem, nestling in the hollow between several hills, and showing a vague picturesque mass of bricks through its heavy pall of smoke. If it were an old Flemish town, beautiful in detail and antiquely interesting, one would say the situation was ideal. It is not beautiful in detail, but the smoke transforms its ugliness into a beauty.[13]

The question as to what source material Bennett was dealing with has been well summarized by Frank Swinnerton, describing the Potteries as "a curiously unchanged society" when Bennett wrote the first of his Five Towns novels, *Anna of the Five Towns* (1902). Swinnerton goes on to say: "Staffordshire, until the end of the eighteenth century, had been as remote from the rest of England as any part of the country could be. Roads were bad; the great ports were all far distant . . . but until the genius of Josiah Wedgwood transformed the industry even Stafford-shire pots were stay-at-home."[14]

It is in Bennett's confrontation with the qualities of narrowness, harsh self-sufficiency, and emotional indifference that a new kind of regional consciousness emerges in these novels. Something about the reserve of his people—which, of course, he found in himself—became a foundation for that particularly English form of regional belonging that tends to create borderlands, demarcates areas of possession, and, most of all, insists that strength in communal success and security comes from being restricted, confined, circumscribed. This is something of infinite interest to the regional writer, as it creates a metaphor for that call of abroad: "Such wind as scatters young men through the world, / To seek their fortunes farther than at home / Where small experience grows," as Shakespeare says in *The Taming of the Shrew*.[15]

At the core of Bennett's Five Towns identity is the urge to escape the pull of home and the partially sympathetic account of those whom home has shaped. In *Anna of the Five Towns* we have a representative novel in this respect: Bennett makes her the very epitome of the individual almost deprived of identity by her domineering father. Yet it is more than this: what Ephraim represents in an extreme form is the person totally shaped and defined by a place and a moral system. His miserliness and his self-imposed prison of routine leads Anna to be subsumed into his nature for the greater part of the book. Bennett sets up what has to be sloughed off, then provides the antithesis of place, the Isle of Man representing what the Five Towns cannot offer.

Anna, in her spiritual crisis, forgets to buy meat and to do household chores. On her return, knowing that her father will be in a bad temper, Bennett tells us:

As she entered the house, she felt a tear on her cheek. She was ashamed to weep, but she wept. This, after the fiasco of the prayer-meeting, was a climax of woe; it overtopped and extinguished all the rest; her soul was nothing to her now.[16]

Bennett is at pains to point out that the paralysis of spirit and vitality, the lack of adventurousness so crucial to his protagonists, is notably absent from most dwellers of his places, like Miss Dickinson at the sewing meeting: "She was thirty-five years of age. Twenty of those years she had passed in a desolating routine; she had existed in the midst of life and never lived."[17]

With Bennett, we have the first novelist of genius in English who understands the paradox of the regional consciousness: a microcosm one may control and yet also a stultifying place where moral and ideological imperatives may paralyze the individual. He makes it clear that Anna is able to see a certain beauty in her environment and that she admires the more enterprising ones, but the fact that she inherits £50,000 and yet hands her cash and bank-books over to her father speaks volumes about the cramping existential *Angst* of the provincial mind. Duty rules everything, and Bennett's towns have the quality of enervating those who give in to the siren-like comforts of the diurnal round. To live at the far end of Trafalgar Road, we are told, "was the final ambition of many citizens."[18]

The Clayhanger trilogy is an extension of these themes. Edwin Clayhanger was "splendidly serious" and full of humor and life. But the generational conflict occurs, again, at the heart of the grip of the place and its moral strictures and self-help philosophy. What can irritate is the smallness of the ambitions of the characters. D. H. Lawrence saw Anna as a poor soul with very moderate aims and a rather mechanical life on the page, but essentially one of the strengths of Bennett's writing on the Five Towns is the evocation of the astonishing beauty of the industrial landscape, used as an integral part of the characters' moods. Work is at the center of this; Bennett is often at his best when explaining and describing the relation between humanity and workplace. In this respect he is as adept at using environment as is Hardy. Describing Ephraim's spare office, for instance:

The principal things in it were an old oak bureau and an old oak desk-chair which had come to him from his first wife's father. . . . A safe stood in a corner opposite the door.[19]

In contrast, Price's workplace at his shambling pottery is vital and integral to his involvement in life:

Decrepit doorways led to the various shops on the ground floor; those on the upper floor were reached by narrow wooden stairs, which seemed to cling insecurely to the exterior walls. Up one of these stairways Mr. Price climbed with heavy, elephantine movements.[20]

Bennett worked into his narratives of escape the now familiar mixture of nostalgia and criticism inherent in the notion of the small town mind-set. But he was writing about a region that had been subject to massive and rapid social change, and he had to use his fictional material in a way that reflected his own ambiguity.

THE KAILYARD AND SCOTTISHNESS

Almost all reference books enter their comments on the Kailyard School of novelists with a tone of critical negativity. The usual adjectives are clustered around the notions of sentimentality and stereotypes and insist that the novels of S. R. Crockett, J. M. Barrie, and Ian McLaren presented gross misrepresentations of Scottish life that were demolished by George Douglas Brown's *The House with the Green Shutters* (1901). It all seems a neat pattern of attack and riposte, but it is worth recalling the peculiar boom in the readership for Scottish themes generally in the 1890s, and it is worthwhile to relate this in order to understand the emergence of the Kailyard writers.

Between ca. 1890 and the Glasgow Empire Exhibition of 1938, in spite of the Scottish Literary Renaissance, the persistence of the Highlander and Burns myths as invented regional versions of Scottishness is remarkably stable and firmly stuck in the Scotland of the imagination found in Queen Victoria's Balmoral, Landseer's paintings, and Scott's novels. This is all the more remarkable because it is well documented that the harsh Highland clearances continued until the late 1840s. Ian Maxwell has pointed out that "Eviction was so rampant in 1848 and 1849 that [it led to] the unsettling of the foundations of the social system."[21]

R. L. Stevenson was, of course, using Scottish history in his fiction before the 1890s Kailyard writers, but whereas he was using folk traditions in his stories and high adventure in his children's books, by the last few years of the century Scottish identity had been subject to a cultural crusade for supposed Highland virtues and rural simplicity that looked back to Scott's domestic and bookish characters. In the journal *Literature*, for instance, in the issue for 17 September 1898, the leader, "The Heritage of Burns," welcomes the supposed decline of Kailyard writing and puts the blame on the heritage of Burns: "But one who grows up into a ready-made literary atmosphere must have an uncommon strength of mind if he is to resist all the influences he feels, and to write differently from everyone around him. And the overwhelming tendency in Scottish literature is towards what is provincial and parochial."[22]

Literature had pretensions to being highbrow and cosmopolitan, and its castigation of Scottish writing for being primarily interested in Scotland seems harsh; but the piece blames the talent of Burns and Scott for causing Scottish writers to stick to the familiar inventions of kilt and bothy when the world had moved on considerably.

Despite these Anglocentric distortions, the Kailyard remains one of the clearest examples of British regional writing, with an agenda to celebrate Scottish life and character, often through historical perspectives, but by means of an emotional, community-centered literature that is deliberately small-scale—the term "Kailyard" from the Scottish "kale," meaning cabbage, denoting a cabbage patch, a backyard, a doorstep focus for stories.

Two works may be taken as representative: J. M. Barrie's memoir of his mother, *Margaret Ogilvy by Her Son* (1897), and S. R. Crockett's novel, *Cleg Kelly* (1896). Barrie's book was an astonishing success; but, as Andrew Birkin comments: "The praise was not universal. Many Scottish critics felt that family privacy had been violated, while Barrie's own family—in particular his elder brother Alexander—alleged that Barrie had exaggerated his humble origins."[23]

The memoir is more than warmly affectionate; it openly explores the family grieving on the death of Barrie's younger brother. But more prominently, it provides a template for the concerns of the Kailyard, in that it celebrates the homely, the manners and mores of the microcosm of region, and it indirectly gives an apologia for the high level of sentiment found in this writing. The basis of this is often in the remarks about Barrie's developing career and his mother's involvement and support. She was the source of his Auld Lichts stories, and the book gives an account of his departure into new subjects, mainly in the world of journalism. But what increasingly dominates both the tone and the subject of the book is the nature of his mother as a tutelary deity of Kailyard ideology. This is seen clearly in the chapter "A Day of Her Life," in which we have the fine detail of her qualities of industry, commitment to family, and economy. Barrie even gives an encomium of her appearance:

She is up now, and dressed in her thick maroon wrapper; over her shoulders (lest one should stray despite our watchfulness) is a shawl, not placed there by her own hands, and on her head a delicious mutch (and the dirge of the elaborate black cap) from the day when she called witchcraft to her aid and made it out of snow-flakes, and the dear worn hands that washed it tenderly in a basin.[24]

Her life is all sewing, cooking, and reading the New Testament and improving books generally.

The majority of critics tend to agree that the Auld Lichts stories of Barrie and the works of Ian Maclaren and S. R. Crockett suffer from an extreme sentimentality that erases any sense of authentic historical vision, despite the presence of the Kirk, the bothy, and the master–servant issues so prominent in the social context of the novels, which mostly tend to be historical. *Cleg Kelly* purports to deal with the life and adventures of a street urchin and criminal, and the chapters dealing with the social origins of his debased character are often impressive in their pace and interest, but the attempt at naturalism comes closer to Disney than being anywhere near such writing as Robert Louis Stevenson's short stories. It might be lamented that Stevenson never fully developed his contemporary Scottish material, despite the power of his essays and short stories.

Crockett's tale has a superfluity of embellishment, and this is in sub-Dickensian style. His convention is that of the verbose raconteur, using the narrative of the omniscient author to elucidate both social problems and individual enterprise and "character," as when Cleg takes over a wooden hut (his father is in jail at this point) and Crockett has him appeal to Callendar, the builder:

"If ye please sir," he said, "they turned me oot at the brickyard and I brocht the bits o' things here. I kenned ya wadna send me away Maister Callendar."

"How kenned ye that I wadna turn ye away boy?" said the builder.

"Oh I just preferred to come back here at ony rate," said Cleg.

"But why?" persisted Mr. Callendar.

Cleg scratched the turned-up earth of his garden thoughtfully with his toe.

"Weel," he said, "If ye maun ken, it was because I had raither lippen to the deil I ken, than to the deil I dinna ken."[25]

Crockett exemplifies that tendency of the Kailyard writers to offer deliberate, blandly extended explanatory prose that distinguishes that variety of regional writing that misrepresents. The distortion is, para-doxically, almost ironical. But in the end, as T. M. Devine has written, these writers "committed the unforgivable sin of being hugely success-ful by publishing a number of best-sellers for the home as well as the vast Scottish expatriate market."[26]

When George Douglas Brown, in *The House with the Green Shutters* (1901), presented the community of Barbie as a place packed with petty hatreds and a prevalent ideology of acquisitiveness and materialism, he was at pains to destroy the Kailyard. But the issue of constructing a region, as it were, from outside, from exile, and from a position of that desire to create myth so dominant in local belonging becomes a central organizing principle in the massively influential regional texts of the Modernist period, and Brown's book is discussed in the next chapter in the context of Joyce's *Dubliners* and Synge's West of Ireland. It took such spinners of myth as Yeats and such cultural nationalists as Saunders Lewis and Hugh MacDiarmid to initiate a totally new litera-ture of regional consciousness.

4

Fin de Siècle

It seems remarkable that there has been so little attention paid to regional writing at the end of the nineteenth century, when such a massive body of biography and criticism has been devoted to regional writing and sense of place in the Romantic and early to mid-Victorian periods. In this instance I refer only to geographical and political boundaries, but this study is concerned with senses of belonging and place in both literal and metaphorical ways. The current interest in borders and frontiers, in imaginative and ideological contexts, is another modern viewpoint on 1890s writing that has not been fully applied yet. My three case studies are intended to show how established ideas of place and region changed in the decade.

James Burnley achieved remarkable success as a Yorkshire writer, at a time when that statement of identity was supported by a vast literature that defined the features of the regional belonging we find in diverse literature, from almanacs to popular fiction and journalism. His book, *The Romance of Modern Industry* (1889) and Charles Forshaw's anthology of Yorkshire poetry, *The Poets of Keighley, Bingley and Haworth* (1891), testify to the profound interest in the wealth-making possibilities of "the North" just as much as to the curiosity about artistic qualities (the Brontës figure in the above anthology, for instance).

Burnley's career represents that intense interest in "the North" that was evident in the fin de siècle cultural setting. As historians such as Keith Robbins and Helen Jewell have shown, the provincial mind-set was not confined to the vague location of "the North": that term came to represent the essential qualities of the provincial.[1]

The second text is Arthur Morrison's collection of short stories, *Tales of Mean Streets* (1894). For various reasons, a revisionary assessment of this collection is due. The achievement here is remarkable, and as a case study in the literature of the underclass, so prominent in that decade, the book provides interesting material on the blurred boundaries between the terms "regional," poetry of place, and metropolitan writing.

The framework of borders, both real and metaphorical, underlies the case studies. Morrison locates his mean streets specifically, as he does the Jago in *A Child of the Jago* (1896), and his work illustrates the nature of placing metropolitan, urban writing very specifically at that time. Arnold Bennett's first novel, *A Man from the North* (1898), for instance, and Somerset Maugham's *Liza of Lambeth* (1897), both pay close attention to particular places. In Bennett's case, he even uses real names. Morrison's work fits with a subgenre of "the abyss," of course, but also stands out as a notable example of revisionary realism, following to some extent the influential Zola.

Morrison's is a fiction of the city and the metropolis—the latter as a state of mind as much as a location. In the twentieth century, we have come to see the city as a central image of Modernism, and now as a key element in the sensibilities we name as "Postmodern" also. Iain Chambers has made this point about the city through modern eyes, and it places Morrison's importance for us: "While the earlier city was a discrete geographical, economic, political and social unit, easily identified in its clear-cut separation from rural space, the contemporary Western metropolis tends towards the drawing of 'elsewhere' into its own symbolic zone."[2]

The new versions of realism need attention, of course, and such genres as narrative of Empire or the romances of Hall Caine needed to define themselves in some way against the recurrent problem of writing satisfactorily about the working class. Morrison, as we know now after P. J. Keating's work, had working-class origins, and his writing about the East End differs significantly from the viewpoint and aesthetics of George Gissing in *The Nether World* (1889). I shall follow this contrast.[3]

The important point about Morrison's stories is that they foreshadow the later writing about the working class that we find, for instance, in James Hanley's *Boy* (1931). There is a directness and a lack of overt stylistic artifice in the stories. There is also a visible effort to play down the moralistic or even the broader contextual elements beyond the claustrophobic world of the mean streets. In the end, we are forced to consider the notion of meaningful community, or its absence; the once commonly held view that there was no community in England—simply an aggregation, and a disintegrating one at that—needs attention, given Morrison's imploding community, in which a thief can leave a revival meeting and rob a blind street-vendor of her few pennies, or in which violence against women is accepted practice.

After all, it was in another seminal fiction of the decade in question, H. G. Wells's *The Time Machine* (1895), that his dystopia is dominated by the Morlocks—genetic extensions of the current workers building the underground. That central Victorian painting of "Work," showing the noble, muscular navvies building a road, being watched approvingly by Thomas Carlyle, seems a massive negative irony alongside Wells's vision, and also when compared to the unemployed workmen of Morrison's story, "Without Visible Means." The working class were at this time, of course, viewed in post-Darwinian terms and always with the current fears of anarchy and rebellion in mind—so the question remains, how should they be represented in fiction? For James Burnley in his journalism, they are gentle, humorous, bland. For Morrison, they are a mix of victim and beast. As for Housman—there the working class is a "lad" who ploughs but also murders and tends to become cannon-fodder: both heroic and pathetic.

These two case studies reveal a great deal about the notions of center and "difference" in literary studies; they construct aspects of that sense of place which we have often tended to romanticize (as in the case of John Clare, for instance) when reading from a distance, in all senses. But they also disclose certain tendencies in metropolitan and nonmetropolitan writing that persist today. We need to look again at those figures who came to represent the central consciousness of the 1890s, perhaps seeing them as being not necessarily metropolitan but peripheral. After all, Francis Thompson was born in Preston, went to school in Durham, and saw the metropolis from the gutter initially, not from the drawing room and the restaurant. One of the first biographies of him, that by John Thomson in 1912, is called *Francis Thompson the Preston-Born Poet.*[4]

Robin Young has made high claims for this revisionary look at the writers at the margins:

At other times the only way of evoking a true sense of the relationship between an age and its deepest cultural intelligences may be to explore the tensions between established taste (the picture which the controlling forces in society wish to project themselves) and the isolated truth-tellers—those who contrive to give a truer picture, or keep alive the deepest values of the societies at whose margins they work.[5]

Yet there is also a sense of other "borders" in these case studies. The binary oppositions of city and land, sophistication and simplicity, wealth and poverty, home and rootlessness are crucially important in understanding the writing of the 1890s, but there is also that border of a more individual yet universal nature. This is the sense of self, of personal fulfillment, and of belonging in one's own time. A. E. Housman's poems in *A Shropshire Lad* are about a great many subjects, but one profound sensibility they express is the imagined homeland, the geography of childhood, and of an ideal of a place—in this instance of a rural England. But this longing for the place, for the imagined topography of happiness and self-knowledge, is not satisfied. The poems do evoke the "blue, remembered hills," but they do so from a position of impossibility. Undoubtedly, this sense of exclusion mirrors Housman's homosexuality and his position at the margins of society, in spite of his professorship and status of respect.

Housman represents the tendency to understand the important and meaningful through loss. Edward Thomas, looking with hindsight on the fin de siècle urban condition, writes about this loss in terms of meeting an old man who tells his life story—a cycle of youth on the land and maturation as a clerk in the city:

He concluded by saying that he had had ten years in that house and those woods, that then his father died, he went away to school and afterwards into an office. Those ten years were the only reality in his life. Everything since had been heavy illusion without rest.[6]

The three case studies, then, represent an important aspect of those varieties of region and belonging that create much of the 1890s consciousness in the writers. The dominance of London on the literary scene, and its magnetic charm for aspiring young writers, meant that both the attraction and the shortcomings of the provinces had somehow to be explained. When the hero of Bennett's *A Man from the North*, Richard Larch, has to return home to the Potteries for a family funeral, we have a standard picture of these regional reductions of self-identity. Richard avoids the main streets because he imagines a meeting with an acquaintance:

> He foresaw the inevitable banal dialogue:
>   "Well, how do you like London?"
>   "Oh, it's fine!"
>   "Getting on all right?"
>   "Yes thanks."
> And then the effort of two secretly bored persons to continue a perfunctory conversation unaided by a single mutual interest.[7]

Bennett here reflects his own experience of meeting the artistic society of London, sensing its vibrancy and self-confidence. The 1890s literature provides ample evidence of this metropolitan allure. Perhaps the best-known example of the subject came with James Joyce's 1904 collection, *Dubliners,* in which the story "A Little Cloud" develops the idea even more, to the extent of having his character Chandler imagine himself as a "Celtic Twilight" poet about to impact on London.

In other words, the provincial's dream of the metropolis stands at odds with the civic pride and the aggressive, highly mediated regional consciousness that we find in James Burnley and his like. Ironically, Burnley himself was to move to London by the 1890s, going into higher journalism in the age of the bookman.

JAMES BURNLEY AND BRADFORD

In the late nineteenth century there was a widespread flowering of local writing, often in the vernacular, and sometimes in remarkably original and vibrant dialect. It was a period in which local and regional publishing was burgeoning, and it was not difficult for an earnest middle-class amateur poet to bring his or her work into print. The sense of local belonging was mediated to all classes, however, and the literature of the time shows this awareness on the part of the publishers that they should cater for all tastes.

It is in Bradford, perhaps more than in any other Victorian city, that the literary culture around the new aspirations to read and write both high-quality literature and popular narratives is apparent. There are many reasons for this: the influx of German immigrants who brought their love of higher cultural pursuits; the appeal of a bohemian, cosmopolitan culture to the new middle class and, most of all, to the energy of individuals. In Bradford, there was a "nest of singing birds" gathered around various clubs, coffee houses, and societies, and a key figure in this was the writer and journalist, James Burnley.

The time was right for such a figure to emerge. Local civic pride was developing in step with the legislation for incorporation (Bradford being made a County Borough in 1889) and with the establishment of literary and philosophical societies such as those thriving in Leeds and Hull in the mid-Victorian years. As Asa Briggs puts it when comparing Bradford with Leeds: Bradford was the first of the two communities to sponsor a handsome new public building that was designed to "elevate" taste and meet the "cultural needs of a business metropolis," and also, with St. George's Hall, as Briggs points out: "What happened inside it was to raise the tone of society also."[8]

A fundamental part of this Bradford culture, though, was in the people, not simply in the buildings and grand public gestures of politicians. Writing was becoming a booming local cultural product, offering outlets for the mediocre enthusiast and the genuine creative spirit. James Burnley was at the heart of this, as editor, poet, comedian, and serious social commentator. As it has often been pointed out, the authors being published could range from clergymen to anonymous operatives on the factory floor. Burnley came on the literary scene with a few poems and a knowledge of the London theater in the 1860s, and he soon became involved with the group of writers around the *Bradford Observer* and *Bradford Review*.

Several writers of later years have commented on the cultural richness and diversity of late-Victorian Bradford, so it is not difficult to imagine the context in which Burnley thrived. W. Riley, for instance, in his autobiography, notes: "Good reference libraries were close at hand; good lectures were available; cultured men and women were ready to stimulate and encourage the serious student. As I recall to mind the opportunities that then presented themselves I appropriate to myself the well-known line of Wordsworth: 'Bliss was it in that dawn to be alive'."[9]

Peter Holdsworth has pointed out the importance of this setting for the young J. B. Priestley, commenting that "in his youth Bradford was . . . culturally dynamic. Theater, literary pursuits, sport and the visual arts thrived alongside a host of societies."[10]

But in the earlier period, when Burnley arrived, there was a notable difference to the more institutionalized developments of fin de siècle Bradford. The writing was more directly comprehensive, aware of working men who wanted good literature as well as supplying the needs of the articulate, leisured middle class who wanted theater reviews and bookish *belles lettres*. Burnley had such a wide range of writing ability that he could fit in with the drinkers and workers at Thomas Nicholson's eating house in Kirkgate, talking to almanac writers and singers, but also dine with the large-scale entrepreneurs, whose lives he was to chronicle in his best-selling book, *The Romance of Modern Industry* (1889).

Burnley was born in Shipley in 1842 and began his long publishing career with a volume of poems, *Idonia and Other Poems* (1869), but his talents extended to other compositions, such as plays, sketches, travel writing, fiction, and journalism. He became most celebrated as "the Saunterer"—the man who produced the almanac *The Saunterer's Satchel* throughout the last decades of the century—and also well known for his "sketches" books: *Phases of Bradford Life* (1871) and *West Riding Sketches* (1875). These two books illustrate the special qualities that made Burnley central to this Bradford literary culture: his mix of serious commentary and understanding humor and his ability to embrace the range of cultural reference from folklore to modern industrial processes. In fact, his most successful books celebrated the woolen industry and the wider Victorian preoccupations with rags-to-riches themes in the age of Samuel Smiles and self-help. His book *The History of Wool and Wool-Combing* (1889) appears to have made his name nationally and gave him access to the drawing-rooms of the wealthy.

What defines Burnley's importance to Bradford writing and to the massive success of the whole group of journalists and poets around him is his local publishing achievements, largely with the founding of *The Yorkshireman* in 1875, initially as a monthly. In later years, as one memoirist puts it, he resided in London "and made a host of friends among the leading literati of the metropolis."[11] In other words, here we have a writer who was one of a class who succeeded in the wake of the huge ocean liner that was dominating the literature of the age: the tugs and supply-boats of the scene. Burnley was very much the "bookman" of the time, as depicted by Walter Besant: "a good steady man of letters . . . this man . . . goes to his study every morning as regularly as a barrister goes to chambers. He finds on his desk two or three books waiting for review, a ms sent for his opinion, a book of his own to go on with."[12]

But for the student of Yorkshire writing, his importance is illustrated when we look more closely at the nature of his almanac, *The Saunterer's Satchel*. Here is a publication that stands out in its time. The almanac, as established in the working-class author tradition, notably in Barnsley, Halifax, and Leeds, had been primarily a calendar with anniversaries, a vehicle for local advertisers (mainly of patent medicines), and perhaps the first type of publication supplying local dialect verse and narrative that provided sustenance for the local and civic pride so foregrounded in the literature and art of the period. The most celebrated almanac, John Hartley's *Clock,* exemplifies this. The average issue contained humor, anecdotes, and rhymes, all very much to the popular taste and similar to the material in demand for Penny Readings and for dialect recitals such as those given by Ben Preston following afternoon tea and Bible classes. The success of Penny Readings was obviously a factor. London publishers—notably Frederick Warne—were producing hardback volumes for these readings by the 1870s.

Burnley's *Satchel* is something else entirely. A typical issue would contain a preface in a chatty tone, a comic drama set in Yorkshire, songs and rhymes in dialect and in Standard English, and fiction. Burnley also introduced an "Answers to Correspondents" column and local news items. These were to continue in the more ambitious *Yorkshireman*. But what defines the difference between the *Satchel* and its competitors is the literary allusions and parodies it included. For instance, we have "A Kersmas Tale—*Not* by Munchausen" and rhymes "not by Poe." In one rhyme, "Sing the Song of the Fleece," Burnley calls the sections of the poem "fyttes," so referring to medieval forms. All this indicates that his readership was a mix of people who simply wanted racy and farcical tales and the middle-class aspirants who read "good literature" and would know a parody when they read it. Even more impressive was the local and topographical nature of the references squeezed into the rhymes, such as, "Of Alpacas superb in which Salts are investors / Of the fleece of the goat from the wilds of Angora / Which makes such sweet dresses for Florry and Dora."

The contents and tone of the *Satchel* indicate that Burnley was keenly aware of the readership, and that the keynote was entertainment. Repeatedly, his prefaces stress the content as "puns quite a sea for jokers facetious to dabble in" and "stories fantastic and stories sarcastic." His aim is always to promote writers "who've been rangers in regions sublime; whose pens, by heaven nourished, give forth ... grand thoughts for all time." In a remarkable typescript written by Burnley late in life, "Literary Recollections of Bradford 1870–1890," he summarizes the groups of literati around Bradford at the time. These would be the writers who supplied copy to the whole range of magazines, almanacs, and newspapers of the area. Burnley lists the main figures: "and into this haunt would occasionally stray for mind-communion John James, the historian of Bradford, for he frequently visited the town he had made famous; Robert Storey, the Craven poet, Ben Preston, Stephen Fawcett, James Hird and others, with mine host Nicholson, smoking his long pipe, presiding."[13]

In his *Phases of Bradford Life*, in which Burnley collected many of his local writings, he has a piece on "Coffee House Life," and this makes clear exactly what it was like to be involved in this "mind-communion": "Here in Bradford there still exist coffee-rooms where discussions on the topics of the day constitute a special feature, and where almost any night may be heard debates equal in vigour, if not in ability, to any heard within the walls of the House of Commons."[14]

He writes of "Straycock's Temperance Hotel" in a dingy court of Kirkgate and has gentle fun at the expense of the crowd of regulars. Even more pastiche and satire is injected into "Barnacle's Evening Party," a sketch in which the Pickwick Club is echoed. The guest list is an exaggeration of the range of writers who perhaps really gathered in the Bradford circle of the time. They include such worthies as "Abimelech Flavonius de Smithkins, the great local author and historian of Wibsey Slack" and "Mr. Silvanio, the tragedian." Barnacles provides his guests with a selection of literature at the party, and this includes: "Long Yarns by an Old Spinner—A Most Amusing Volume" and "Looming in the Distance—A Three-volume Novel by the Author of *Fell'd at Last.*"

There were some remarkable characters in the circle around Burnley, and their enthusiasm and high level of literary appreciation is typified by J. Arthur Binns, whom Burnley describes thus:

But in those years of the late sixties and early seventies he was a man of some leisure and disclosed to me a mind better stored with literary knowledge than that of any men I have ever known. . . . He was chairman of the library committee of the old Mechanics' Institute. He knew the poets so thoroughly that he had many of their best pieces literally off by heart. He could recite the whole of Pope's Essay on Man, and reel off poems and stanzas from Shelley.[15]

To Bradford generally he was known as the president of the Third Equitable Building Society.

The Poets of Bingley, Keighley and Howarth (1891), a volume edited by another Bradford literary man, Charles Forshaw, gives an insight into the whole community of writers of all shades: poetasters, neo-Romantics, hack journalists, and wealthy amateurs. The volume was financed by subscription, and the list of subscribers reflects the sheer diversity of creative people around Burnley. There are no fewer than twenty-nine local publications listed, largely poetry collections and anthologies of local writing. Burnley himself, in his contribution to the book (on James Hird), says something that defines the spirit behind this Bradford literary circle: "As Mr. Hird advanced to manhood he forced himself into a better career than the mill had offered him, and by dint of self-culture and perseverance was able to take up a position . . . that yielded him greater opportunities . . . for the expansion of his mind and the exercise of his poetic gifts."[16]

A remarkable feature of this literary culture was that, as time went on, links were made with other towns. John Hartley was involved, and when a Yorkshire Literary Union was formed in April 1870, there was a notable insistence on the importance of a body of "Yorkshire literature" forming an important part of the consciousness of how people belonged to this region, with a sense of place and identity that sustained a massive publication program for decades. Burnley insists on the general camaraderie in addition to an interest in literature. He writes: "It must not be imagined that the Bradford writers did not chum together socially as well as in literary matters. . . . There was a strain of Bohemianism about some of us." He clearly hankered for a mix of café society and serious literary production, and his works reflect this diversity.

As the focal achievement in all this endeavor was undoubtedly the writing of dialect literature with an intention of treating it as more than a novelty, it has to be stressed that the dramas, tales, and poems in *The Yorkshireman* and in the *Satchel* represent a genuine attempt to depict the authentic domestic and laboring lives of people in the area. The drama owes a great deal to the London tradition of burlesque as written by such satirists as Cruikshank, but there is not always an avoidance of sentimentality in the writing. When the realism is successful, there is an attempt to present the vernacular with care in terms of phonetic accuracy, giving the writing a genuine feel. It also creates the shared humor that a magazine constructs with reader and writer, as initiated by Addison and Steele with the early-eighteenth-century *Spectator*. After all, this was the era in which dialect writers were beginning to attract large audiences and had reading circuits and substantial volumes of their work published. Edwin Waugh (1817–1890) typifies this, surviving as a full-time writer. The tradition of selling pamphlets and booklets in the streets was still continued. The establishment in 1877 of the English Dialect Society suggests just how much interest in this literature had developed by the time of Burnley's publications.

In 1889 Burnley stepped up to become an amateur sociologist and business correspondent. In this he moved from historian of folk culture to the celebration of success, of the puritan work ethic, and of the transformation effected by wealth and social status. The basis of his inquiry into the success of men such as Titus Salt, Cunliffe Lister, and Isaac Holden is that "Romance and industry have long been regarded in the popular mind as things apart" and that "The imagination is always impressed by stories of men who have carved their way from obscurity to wealth."

Burnley's work in Bradford has a greater significance than it has been given. As a writer and a propagandist for social progress and the amelioration of the condition of man through work and cultural fulfillment, Burnley surely deserves to be reread. His writings provide valuable evidence of important social and cultural history; but far more important than this is his place in the chronicles of both an emerging working-class interest in literature and the middle-class acquisition of the "higher culture" of the upper classes. All this came at a time when English literature was only just in the process of becoming recognized as a subject with meaning and status. But it was the Bradford setting and its unique contributions to the new publishing enterprises that gave Burnley his real break as a writer. As he put it in his introduction to *West Riding Sketches*: "In the West Riding . . . the old and new clash together so indiscriminately, the prose and the poetry intermingle so curiously, that it requires one to be 'native' and 'to the manner born' to distinguish the lines of demarcation."[17]

Burnley was very much the creation of the emergence of regional consciousness born of civic pride, and the writers in his circle certainly understood that Yorkshire was an entity as part of a concept of "the North," and that it was also a state of mind, and it needed a literature of its own, largely to counteract the stereotypes given it by London writers.

In helping to cultivate these things in and around Bradford, Burnley was more than simply a jobbing literary man. He and his Bradford friends never produced anything that did not have its foundation in an affection for the city. In the final words of his recollections, he says: "Of course, every decade does not give Bradford a Ben Preston, or a Broughton, or a Robbins . . . still with the encouraging examples of those twenty years to look back upon, there ought to be incentive enough to budding literary talent to put forth its highest endeavors in advancing the literary reputation of this good old town."[18] How right he was. In the decade after Burnley's time there, a young J. B. Priestley was talking shop in the Swan Arcade and reading the almanacs.

A study of James Burnley's achievement in Bradford surely confirms to the literary historian that he should perhaps look more closely at how regional writing did more than simply ape a Dickens or a Trollope. The careers of the whole circle around him illustrate that there was much more to them as writers than merely a talking shop of dilettantes.

ARTHUR MORRISON AND *TALES OF MEAN STREETS*

According to recent critical writing on the life and writing career of Arthur Morrison (1863–1945), an assessment of his achievement and attempts to "place" him in the history of working-class writing have been difficult. This has been because he never helped to establish reliable facts and also because his career faded after the turn of the century, as he gave more time to his interest in Japanese art.

Even as late as 1967, in the updated edition of Legouis and Cazamian's extensive *History of English Literature,* he merits the shortest of footnotes as an author of the "realist and social novel."[19] But now we have bibliographical summaries, new editions of his classic *A Child of the Jago* (1896), and fresh critical interest. For the present study, the story collection, *Tales of Mean Streets*, has been chosen, for several reasons. In order to explain this, a short digression is needed, placing the book in the thematic importance given here.

These stories are remarkable for several reasons, not least for the peculiar focus on a minimal viewpoint in the narrative technique on simple externals. Zola's doctrine of naturalism has been seemingly reduced to the very minimum required for the reader's immediate understanding of causality and physical being. In the history of writing about the working classes in Victorian fiction, *Tales of Mean Streets* has a unique position, and it is largely for this reason, based on technique. One only has to read the opening paragraph of the first story, "Lizerunt," alongside Elizabeth Gaskell's *Mary Barton*, published fifty years previously, to see the difference in treatment. Gaskell loads the descriptions with sentimental, distancing statements when she writes of the Davenports in the Manchester cellar, members of the unemployed underclass at starvation point: "Her little child crawled to her, and wiped with its fingers the thick-coming tears which she now had strength to weep."[20] Here, the language overloads with detail, and emotive words draw out what should be easily inferred by the reader. The opening of "Lizerunt," in contrast, tells us that "her cheeks were very red, her teeth were very large and white, her nose was small and snub, and her fringe was long and shiny." When Lizerunt suffers violence, we have simply: "Lizer strained and squalled, 'Le' go! You'll kill me an' the kid too!' She grunted hoarsely."

Even if we look at George Gissing's contemporary book on a comparable subject, *The Nether World* (1889), the difference in the sheer density of adverbial and adjectival qualification and enlargement of the subjects described is notable.[21] I am stressing these in order to pinpoint Morrison's extraordinary style in these respects: he drains all extraneous matter from the fiction, assembling a series of sketches of the life in the streets and houses of the East End using many methods we now label "Modernist."

The present focus, however, is to draw attention to the place of the collection in the context of region and belonging. In fact, as a case study it illustrates what was becoming a central concern of 1890s writers and poets: a new variety of rootlessness within a meaningless microcosm in a state of subjectivity to market forces. The essential elements of this scene—familiar in fin de siècle studies—are the massive expansion in the commuter–metropolitan class, the new literacy since the 1870 Education Act had forced out the uneducated, the creation of fringe subcultures existing on the poverty-line, and the threat to stability offered by the new proletariat. The social history of the decade tells us of outrageous disparities in the quality of life in Britain's hub of empire. The twin narratives of empire in the wider world and the "Darkest England" genre only serve to emphasize even more the nature of the dispensable, the unvalued masses. In modern social and critical theory, writers have extended this into writing about "war and population control." Margot Norris, for instance, says: "The Victorian coding of the masses as proletarian was transferred to the mass formations of World War I battlefields, which with their physical configurations of muddy, filthy, polluted trenches were easily figured in the public imagination as industrial slums."[22] In other words, Morrison's collection is indeed about "region and belonging" in that it demolishes the notion. The fiction negates every concept that had been established in Victorian writing about the sense of community after the second wave of the Industrial Revolution and the move into the new towns. In that sense, Gaskell's depiction of the starving in the basements and Dickens's Stephen Blackpool are part of this antidote to the mythic literature of idealistic community under crown and empire.

By 1890, the missionaries were entering the East End, of course, and so were the creative writers, looking for the "other England" beyond what had come to be defined as "civilization." Arthur Morrison is an interesting case in this context: a working-class writer who really was born into that class, despite his later social mobility. He was born in Poplar, the son of an engine-fitter, and his work with the People's Palace in the Mile End Road gave him a close knowledge of the streets and people he fictionalized.

There is a modern documentary feel about the collection, but essentially the thirteen stories are strong, socially aware narratives hinging on varieties of love and attachment. But these patterns of urban relationships negate the norms of mainline popular fiction of the time. Seven stories deal explicitly with couples in marriage or courtship; four focus on lesser forms and influences of capitalism, and one in particular, "The Red Cow Group," is political comedy. What the stories have in common is a constant inquiry as to the failure of a nascent society to comprehend and protect all its members. The close focus constantly reinforces the view that there is a distant system that excludes and callously discards those forgotten by mechanisms that lead to power through wealth.

Every story concerns a victim of some kind; there is a bias toward males as the causes of disorder and aggression. Women are denigrated and abused at every opportunity, yet it is also women who provide the strength for the most optimistic glimpses of survival in this underworld. There is no moral viewpoint. Even the story containing the most obvious version of escape, "Squire Napper," in which the protagonist inherits wealth, makes it clear that the men in the mean streets only have a capacity for sensual indulgence and instant gratification.

But the dominant writing method is to close up and exclude the wider metropolitan context. The only belonging is the dependence on the family unit as a survival mechanism. The story that illustrates this most clearly is "Behind the Shade." This concerns the Perkins women— mother and daughter—who try to survive by a cultural acquisition at odds with the environment: they offer piano lessons. From the opening, they are odd. Mrs. Perkins has suffered a violent assault and yet is thought to have deserved this, as she was a "churchgoer." Even their house is distinguished and so is a subject for obloquy:

Although the house was smaller than the others, and was built upon a remnant, it was always a house of some consideration. In a street like this mere independence of pattern gives distinction.[23]

The two women place an advertisement for piano lessons, and "It was not approved by the street." After their failure, and an absence of communication with the neighborhood, the bodies of the women are found: "Both deaths, the doctor found, were from syncope, the result of inanition."

What develops increasingly as the stories progress is a composite image of a working-class community that undermines previously accepted assumptions about "regional" and communal identity. Arguably, in the mid-Victorian period, certain views of the proletariat as undergoing a developmental enlightenment were expressed. Class and community were often idealized. The 1849 Select Committee on Public Libraries, for instance, as Lewis C. Roberts has shown, asserted an optimism about the workers: "The working class was depicted throughout the Report as both fit for and in need of institutions to provide them with good books. The Committee found 'a great improvement in the national habits and Manners' of the working class and concluded that the people would be able to appreciate and enjoy . . . Public Libraries."[24]

The idealizations of the stalwart workers, often genial Joe Gargerys, have no place in Morrison's microcosm. Culture, as defined by the liberal progressive outlook, has no place in the mean streets. In

"Lizerunt," for instance, the Whit Monday fair on Wanstead Flats illustrates what the meager cultural pursuits mean for the men: "you may be drunk and disorderly without being locked up."

Morrison's introduction, reprinted up to the sixth (1906) edition, sets out explicit features of the bare, utilitarian life of the joyless streets. These workers "do not go to Hyde Park with banners. They seldom fight." Even more indicative of Morrison's intentions is to show that "No event in the outer world makes any impression on this street." In the final paragraph of the introduction, he asks: "Where in the East End lies this street? Everywhere. . . . This street of square holes is hundreds of miles long."

In other words, Morrison's fiction deliberately challenges the idea of a region with constructions of "belonging by negating the concepts of community, and insisting that it is the location in the metropolis that has caused this enervated condition of life." Yet he also departs from the "descent into hell" nature of the subgenre defined by the use of the Dantesque/Dore cultural image of a subhuman underclass in "circles of man-made hell. *Tales of Mean Streets* has no framing device and no narrator/guide. Morrison places the reader very close to the anecdotal figures that make up the narrative device: "Everything, I say, went well enough until Billy bought a ladies' tormentor."[25] The language puts us in the position of listeners to a narrative free from judgment and assessment. We are given facts and events only.

The stories, in their challenge to the assumptions about the working-class community, are purposely anti-Romantic. No claims are made for any notions such as nature or innocence. No image of rural bliss is placed beside the forgotten street life. The bare fact is that this regional self-regard is one only in terms of a sense of exclusion—these people are excluded from the prosperity concomitant with capitalism. Family structures and vestiges of courtship just survive, tenuously, in the midst of an increasingly amoral milieu. It is interesting to note that, in the one story in which the denizens of the mean streets leave the locale to find work, the central event is a robbery of one worker by a traveling "friend." In this story, "Without Visible Means," Morrison gives the one impression of a wider world. In the autumn of the "Great Strikes," some men go in search of work. They travel as far as Hatfield and a little beyond, and they live like tramps on the road, with little comfort. On the one occasion when Morrison could have drawn a pastoral contrast, he avoids anything more than a bland, perfunctory sentence: "At Potter's Bar the party halted and sat under a hedge to eat hunks of bread and cheese."[26] From a first phase of false camaraderie, the story develops into a cruel theft at the closure.

Once again, though, the redemption in humanity is through female characters. One man finds three shillings in his bag, put there by his wife. At another point on the trek, a woman gives them a shilling. Repeatedly, in the stories, the ruin inside the community—a kind of emotional implosion—is brought about by the men. Male violence decides power in sexual politics, male labor determines survival or the opposite, and male brutality and amorality cause failure and disillusionment.

There is no patriarchal guidance in the community, no sense of meaningful difference. Escape is through Sunday idleness, the beer shop, and the fights. In all aspects, the community that Morrison depicts cancels out the previous Victorian insistence on perfectibility in man. As a text of the 1890s, *Tales of Mean Streets* has parallels with Gissing, with Hardy in *Jude the Obscure* and *Tess*, and with much of the urban poetry of the London streets, but it also has a firm relationship to the established regional novel. This relationship is one of implied questioning and revaluation. The fiction makes us revise previous ideas of how locality creates a sense of place beyond the functional and economic.

One of the ways in which we can see the exact nature of Morrison's fiction in terms of writing about the working class and the underclass is to compare it to two specific elements in the growth of such literature immediately before *Tales of Mean Streets*. One obvious subject is the use of a local dialect or argot. In the North of England, for instance, extreme orthographic representation of working people's speech was the norm in the hugely popular dialect almanacs such as Burnley's *Saunterer's Satchel*, or John Hartley's *Clock Almanac*. The latter was begun in 1865, and its circulation by 1887 was 80,000; it continued well into the twentieth century. The issues of the 1890s contain images of the working class of the North as generally beneficent, mild, industrious folk. A typical example would be this section from an issue of 1899, concerning a courtship centered on a public house:

"Arthur—Arthur Hemingway is my name. Good morning Miss—Miss Bella—I dooant remember yer tother name."

"Bella will do. And so I've surprised you gathering wild flowers? Are they not lovely? Sometimes I think . . . they are sweeter than those we grow in our garden."

"Varry likely—they are bonny reight enuf—an awm glad yo like 'em. May aw get that bunch for yo?"[27]

The enormous success of this Northern dialect literature is in sharp contrast to the whole category of East End "lower depths" fiction with regard to dialectal representation. Within a few years of Morrison's book, fiction by Maugham, Bennett, and Gissing all contain working-class characters. Gissing, in *The Nether World*, just drops aitches; Bennett makes his clerk in *A Man from the North* simply a stereotype Cockney; Maugham, in *Liza of Lambeth*, stresses the local color, and his speech is close to that of the Doolittles of *Pygmalion*. These are all closer to the Northern dialect writings in this respect than Morrison. In the first chapter of *Liza of Lambeth*, for instance, some girls are dancing, and they see Liza:

"I sy, ain't she got up dossy?" called out the groups at the doors as she passed.
"Dressed ter death, and kill the fashion, that's wot I calls it."[28]

Morrison's slang orthography and vocabulary are close to Maugham's. There was clearly, however, a difference in closeness and instinctive familiarity in Morrison's case. Whatever the differences and similarities, the point is that Morrison's speech is reductive, perfunctory. When his East-Enders speak, it is almost invariably functional, not decorative. When Billy Chope takes his mother's savings in "Lizerunt," his language is simply explanatory of his motives; nothing is wasted on showing his power of homely metaphor or even exaggerating his ability to curse.[29]

The other literary element is the subgenre of the topographical sketch, made popular by Dickens and others in such journals as *Household Words*. The format was basically to write of a purposeful visit to a specific locale in order to produce a mix of documentary and reportage, with a dimension of explaining "unknown" culture. James Burnley made this his specialty. In one of his collections, *A Night with the King of Egypt*, for instance, he spends an evening in a public house to observe a mummers' play. The sketch becomes something close to modern travel-writing, but with a gentle humor in part derived from such comedy as Shakespeare's "low-life" scenes. The reader is made to feel that the whole affair is like Prince Hal visiting Falstaff in Eastcheap. But the Victorian version of this reportage was a genuine expression of regional and topographical exposition. Burnley's sketches are also a celebration of the cultural richness of his chosen places. Once again, Morrison's fiction contains a small element of this: the need to explain the physical environment as if a documentary tone were required. He is always aware that he is writing for those who have not seen these lives at first hand, but he writes with restraint. The usual effect of this is similar to listening to a voice-over on a film while taking in the meaning of the image.

Tales of Mean Streets, then, is a remarkable collection for several reasons. A study of how region and belonging were given meaning and mediated in the Victorian context when rapid social and demographic change brought a new sense of place reveals these stories as being a significant achievement. If the modern city is to be understood as a massive, complex intersection of cultures and origins, always a place of immigration and emigration, then the 1890s are the decade when, arguably, fiction writers looked for expressions of this complexity.

Morrison's contribution stands alongside such collections as Joyce's *Dubliners* and Gaskell's Manchester stories as a literature of people and place within an urban renegotiation of communal belonging. But the collection also anticipates the flowering of working-class writing of the 1930s, when those realignments of family and work-identity within Admass (Priestley's term) and metropolitan restructuring had reached a stage of utter modernity in human terms. *Tales of Mean Streets* is at once a fine achievement in a genre of its time and a universal statement of the interrelationships of place and social identity. The final paradox is that the notion of a "region" as a concept indicating distance from the center—a peripheral concept—can be extended to a type of minority awareness within the metropolis itself. Also, if we read the stories in another way, taking the topography as a version of an "anti-region," it bears out what various commentators saw in London: a disparate set of communities in which the notion of belonging to a community was eroded. The reader is forced to ask where the subscription libraries are, and where the concerts and the popular culture that make up the communal sense. Morrison offers the desperate release of the feast—and there we have a brutal confrontation.

A. E. HOUSMAN AND *A SHROPSHIRE LAD*[30]

There is, of course, a massive body of criticism of Housman in print. Naturally, much of this concerns the relation of his poetry to autobiographical experience. It is an easy matter, for instance, to use a Freudian approach or at least develop an understanding of his work based on his homosexuality, appropriating one specific life and its data to an agenda of modernity and revisionist writing. But I want to look at *A Shropshire Lad* from the viewpoint of what we mean (and have meant) by "regional" and by sense of "belonging": two crucially important terms in the history of British poetry.

It has long been accepted that regional writing in Britain is about much more than the use of locality and historical change to give character to particular writings. The standard, canonical regional novelists—for instance, Hardy, the Brontës, Gaskell, Bennett, and Scott—represent varieties of regional consciousness, some even making strong links between character and environment. What has been notable here is the use of Romantic notions of "Nature" and innocence as integral parts of the regional sensibility. Emily Brontë's characters, for example, speak in the dialect of the Yorkshire–Lancashire border; the language is often related to temperament, belief, and morality, as in the case of Joseph and Ellen Dean.

Nature is centrally significant, of course—think of Egdon Heath in *Far from the Madding Crowd* or the moors around Wuthering Heights. The regional in literature in the Victorian context had become, by the 1890s, recognized as what we would call in modern literary theory a site of appropriation in which Romanticism could be related to notions of place and identity. In such a context, regional writing became a type of text working at two levels: first, it set up a dialectic against the metropolitan, the London identity; then it established a type of difference in which human fulfillment or maturation was more apparent—more apparent because it was more visible.

At a simple level, contrasts of country and city exploit these obvious differences, as Housman does in Poem XLI of *A Shropshire Lad*. Here, he talks about "homely comforters" in his own shire before showing the contrast with London:

> But here in London streets I ken
> No such helpmates, only men;
> And these are not in plight to bear,
> If they would, another's care.

But what Housman really succeeded in doing was to create a "local habitation and a name" for that particular fin de siècle melancholy so evident in the literature in all genres. There was no influential version of prose autobiography established at that date in which the idea of regional belonging as expressed in the novel was carried into universal terms, either documentary or biographical. But Housman creates a shire that could be any English shire, despite the place-names. Scholars of Housman's work have shown that he was inaccurate about the factual basis of his geography—yet the "blue remembered hills" of Poem XL are at once the Malverns and every range of hills for everyone.

Housman, then, constructed a mental and imaginative landscape of post-Romantic feeling in which essentials of a neo-Romantic version of regional belonging were encoded. This version was one of self-projection into place. In this, it is a phenomenological process: the writer observes himself looking and making meanings. Of course, it worked in terms of Bredon. He did indeed become the poet of the borders. Maxwell Fraser's 1939 book on Worcestershire, for instance, has this to say: "Yet it is not one of these far-distant times and wonders that those who stand on Bredon will think as their eyes range over the shining rivers. . . . A. E. Housman caught the true joy of Bredon for all time in *A Shropshire Lad*, where he tells "Here of a Sunday morning / my love and I would lie."[31]

Clearly, the phenomenal success of the collection owes much to a feeling akin to the German *Heimat* or the Welsh *Hiraeth*. English has no single word for this longing. Now, the regional in this sense may, naturally, be metropolitan. The "region" could be the East End. But Shropshire is markedly rural and also a borderland. It is on the Marches. Housman manages to textualize a range of margins at several levels of meaning, and it is in this that the poems of *A Shropshire Lad* are essentially regional, though their author had no special knowledge of the county that would be comparable with, say, Scott's knowledge of the Scottish borderlands.

This notion of being marginal applies at several creative sites of interest. The confluence of all Housman's senses of being peripheral, isolated, and antipathetic to the London around him, and indeed of urban modernity, are evident in the collection. He had been living a quiet, retiring life at his time in the Patents Office; he had been rejected by Moses Jackson and had purposely kept his family at a distance. Housman was marginalized in terms of his sexuality, in his failure at university, and also by his anonymous life among the clerks in the metropolis. Everything Shropshire came to represent for him was perfectly in tune with the spirit of the age, as if his was writing by instinct.

The word "regional" applied to Shropshire equates well with "rural" and is indeed notably different from many other southern counties that were becoming commuter-bases in the last decades of the century. Asa Briggs has noted this trend of suburbanization: "The area of 'Greater London' was still increasing rapidly at the end of the nineteenth century, and the progress seemed relentless. 'I have tried to keep Hornsey (in North London) a village,' the Rector of the parish complained, 'but circumstances have beaten me.'"[32] Briggs goes on to remark that after a rapid growth between 1821 and 1841, Brighton was becoming metropolitan rather than provincial.

From this perspective, Shropshire is clearly representative of a county that is not only a borderland, but dominantly rural—the opposite of suburban, with no commuter base. As Barrie Trinder has shown, Victorian Shropshire was predominantly rural: in the 1881 Census almost 27,000 people from a total population of 248,000 were employed in agriculture. "The only industries were stone quarries, some lime-works and brickyards, a few country tanneries and papermills."[33] In addition to this marginality, the military and imperial themes of the collection also focus on a definite context with a social history that is very much of Housman's time. The King's Shropshire Light Infantry, the regiment of the county, was formed in 1881 after the Cardwell army reforms. Housman's soldier lads would have been a more familiar sight than previously, with the county's involvement in imperial campaigns necessarily making more of a presence of military images in ordinary life. But again, the soldiers of the poems are isolated, doom-ridden figures involved in noble sacrifice. This theme of sacrifice is intimately bound up with the poet–persona in the poems. Housman's original *nom de plume* was Terence Hearsay, the parallel being drawn to Terence, a Greek dramatist exiled in Rome, so suggesting a kind of metropolitan exile of anonymity and marginality.

In fact, his biography shows that Housman's viewpoint, even of the actual topography, was distant and vague, just as his central thought was uncertain, measured largely by a questioning of any purpose to life. He had read and dismissed the argument in W. H. Mallock's book, *Is Life Worth Living?* As Richard Perceval Graves argues, Housman disliked the preciseness of philosophical reasoning.[34] His disposition was always contemplative. His childhood viewpoints of Catshill and Fockbury were exactly the right distance for a construction of self-regarding sadness defined by nature and by place.

The 1890s was an age in which the urban and metropolitan had become the focus of humanity. It was in cities that one saw the issues more clearly, as one saw the extremes. It was an age of documentary, "faction," and fact. The inquiries of the urban sociologists were produced parallel to the new, experimental post-Zola fiction, which was searching for fresh metaphors, narrative structures, and symbolic patternings to cope with the latest version of humanity formed by the mature Industrial Revolution. But there was still the rural base. Arthur Morrison makes it clear that one young woman from the country sang when she first came to the Mean Streets, but that was soon erased from her character.

Yet the country was still within walking distance in this decade, and cattle were still brought into the city to market. Essex and Kent were close, and seasonal work there is rural work, with traditional communities. The simple point here is that something integral to the English temperament had been pinpointed by this remarkable collection, and when Grant Richards produced the second edition, *A Shropshire Lad* was indeed the most celebrated collection of poetry for decades in England.

This reintroduces the familiar examples and arguments concerning the representation of "England" in English writing. I do not intend to discuss all these here, but I want to insist that these constructions have been, substantially, defined by means of a regional consciousness. England as a mental construct is essentially that Anglo-Saxon "shire" of Housman combined with virtues that have become increasingly provincial since the 1890s. I would stress that these *provincial* connotations are not the same as regional ones. In literary terms, regional has always been a shaping, instrumental energy on protagonists and memoirists alike, whereas provincial has suggestions of small-minded, narrow, and inward-looking.

The regional, then, by 1890, had become a formative element in English literature, with writers of the stature of George Eliot and Elizabeth Gaskell declaring that in the nonmetropolitan areas life could be seen more clearly and social change more visibly as the determining force of the age.

Housman primarily destroys this. He makes a group of "shires" that distantly and vaguely form an organizational, power-centered England, which fights wars and has jails, while simple love goes on as it will. His landscape is like a vision that may turn from paradisal to hellish at any moment. In fact, the fringes of the poems are locked into the Victorian imperialist quest, and this, in turn, diminishes the rural elegiac impulse in the neo-Romantic lyrics. At times, when reading the poems, it seems as though what is thought "regional" in is fact simply a stasis, a condition of inanition, a limbo in which the self is waiting a destiny:

> Tis a long way further that Knighton,
>   A quieter place than Clun,
> Where doomsday may thunder and lighten
>   And little 'twill matter to one.

> (conclusion of Poem L)

Housman's lecture, *The Name and Nature of Poetry*, includes this statement: "And I think that to transfuse emotion—not to transmit thought but to set up in the reader's sense a vibration corresponding to what was felt by the writer—is the peculiar function of poetry."[35] In this essay, while admiring poems from a variety of ages and traditions, he repeatedly returns to this definition. At the end of the piece, he talks of a "spring" that "bubbles up." All is related to receptivity—receptivity when the intellect is quiescent. For Housman, the process is a trance, a creative state.

Ultimately, *A Shropshire Lad* is about these multiple states of distance, difference, and marginality, which are produced constantly but most noticeably in particular periods of rapid social change. It is surely no accident that versions of regional consciousness become prominent when massive metropolitan advances and economic forces make the anonymous life more prevalent. Regional belonging at the end of the nineteenth century was a conventional artistic construction that had been appropriated for metaphorical use. In James Burnley, it celebrates a new civic sense of self-regard; in Morrison, it locates a state of absence in all those communal forces we expect in a specified class and place; and in Housman, regional becomes a certain dimension of imagined primal life. This state of being has no concepts of "center" and "periphery"—concepts that are crucial to the modern understanding of minorities in all senses of the word.

Yet in the 1890s English writing was clearly intensely aware of the consequences of the new version of the city and all the generated identities that such a concept gave to its inhabitants. The Romantics had prefigured this, as in Coleridge's meditation poems, for instance, but another eighty years on, feelings of a periphery and "another England" under threat produced a range of creative responses. These responses included an interest in regional publishing by London publishers, as well as those in the regions. *Holroyd's Yorkshire Ballads*, for instance, edited by Charles Forshaw, was published in London by Bell (1892). In the case of Housman, the imagery of an imagined regional belonging has persisted, as notably evident in the many illustrated editions of *A Shropshire Lad*, from the 1940 edition, with engravings, to the Walker Books edition of 1991, with lush watercolors alongside the poems.

A NOTE ON *TESS OF THE D'URBERVILLES*

All the above writers, whose work presents, in a range of modes, the importance of regional consciousness in an age of centralization, offer interesting comparisons with the work of Thomas Hardy. Hardy constantly gives the oppositional forces of tradition and modernity center stage in his fiction. In the context of the 1890s, it was at this point in his career as a novelist that he came to focus more directly on the emotional interactions of past and present as a parallel for personality clashes. The protagonists Jude and Tess from the great novels of the 1890s both have an element of that particular destructive implosion of selfhood that occurs in the grand ideological confrontations of the modern urban and the timeless rural.

Hardy's Wessex is a stage for the enactment of these internal malaises and their reflections in the social conflicts occurring as the new world of communications and business shoves aside the microcosm of village community. The "ache of the modern" in *Tess* is in some ways down to her schooling, her book-learning, and her identity as a product of the new centralization. In *Tess* it is made clear that the vestigial lore of the past and all the clusterings of an oral culture are deeply planted in the novel's human-centered thesis. Tess's mother represents this fading world being left behind by the speed of change and the cash nexus of the agrarian revolution:

Between the mother, with her fast-perishing lumber of superstitions, folklore, dialect, and orally-transmitted ballads, and the daughter, with her trained National teachings . . . there was a gap of two hundred years as ordinarily understood.[36]

Hardy repeatedly makes these worlds confront each other as the novel progresses. He establishes the chaotic domesticity of the Durbeyfields alongside the grand, impersonal dwelling of the D'Urbervilles, and he extends the duality of the wealthy and the deprived to the point at which modernity comes to be defined as noise, metal, and efficiency. The focal scene of the threshing and the hard driving of the cart by Alec give the novel an imprint of a new rhythm in life, something with no time for the peripheral, circumscribed world of Mr. Durbeyfield. Tess was "a fine and picturesque country girl and no more" as a "maiden," and somehow she is made to be an unknowing catalyst, allowing the outside displacing forces to cut her family apart.

For Hardy, regional belonging is usually associated with the condition of the innocent victim, the alluring throwback to a mythic past, but it is the poetry of place itself that really gives his regional writing its genuine power, as recounted in the previous chapter. *Tess* is one of the visionary novels, dealing with the unremitting futurity awaiting Tess's inheritors. Such secondary things as dialect and folk culture seem far removed from her basic *hubris*.

In the context of these other 1890s texts, Hardy's vision of his imaginary distant rural region is one carrying the symbolic weight of all the concepts discussed in the introduction: home, insularity, idyll, and the threat of the new and strange. Where Hardy makes these part of the web of his tragedies, his favorite word, "circumstance," surely sits more easily with Morrison's people. Hardy imagined a regional novel in which all that was fascinating in the receding rurality of England could appear in a poetic myth of a golden land, but one in which strangers had set foot and nothing could be the same again.

5

Renaissance:
Inventing Celts, Cities, and Folk

In the critical corpus on Modernism, there is ample material available to demonstrate the centrality of the city as a metaphor and a realistic basis for writing. Most of the major writers in Britain of the period from around 1890 to around 1930 had to find a way to approach the new phenomenon of the city and everything that it spawned. What has not been fully explored is the place of regional belonging within this revolution in writing: questions such as what part the sense of place played as a counterpoint to the Eliotesque vision of the metropolis or the Conradian sophistication of the modern anarchic mind.

With this in mind, criticism must also be careful not to confirm the simplistic definition of Georgian writing as something purely retrograde and neo-Romantic. Certainly, throughout this period, writing about the countryside and the rural vision of unsophisticated man—as in the writings of Edward Thomas, W. H. Hudson, and Richard Jefferies—is not uniformly elegiac and conservative, with an eye to nostalgia and distortion; on the contrary, it celebrates the regional juxtaposed with place as a metaphor for stability. The point is that the rural writers in this Modernist period were eager to explain what was being lost with the arrival of the new commuter class and the booming media machine that fed their desire for entertainment.

Indeed, one of the sources of Georgian writing was the revisionary interest in the Home Counties and the southern areas, which were becoming weekend territory for many. E. M. Forster's portrait of Leonard Bast in *Howard's End* (1910), for instance, includes his walking and rural interests as part of his Ruskinian ideals of self-improvement by absorbed culture:

Borrow was imminent after Jefferies—Borrow, Thoreau and sorrow. R.L.S. brought up the rear, and the outburst ended in a swamp of books. . . . And Leonard had reached the destination. He had visited the county of Surrey when darkness covered its amenities, and its cosy villas had re-entered ancient night.[1]

The writers whose works Bast reads were clearly influential in directing the generation of the Georgians toward the rural vision and the version of self-knowledge and meditation on being the Romantic that Wordsworthian philosophy had to offer modern man.

However, the first step in understanding the role played by regional belonging in the Modernist period is to establish how the metropolis was textualized, and there is no better place to look than in T. S. Eliot's *The Waste Land* (1922). There is an immense amount of work in print on this poem, of course, but what should be stressed here is the city as a mechanism for erasing the sense of place. A place in the individual human sense of authentic existential meaning is one with a communal nature. The organic pull of home, and the concept of "home" in British culture, has always been small-scale, circumscribed, comfortable. Eliot's city is alien, incomprehensible: he describes a place shrouded in fog, and he is overcome by the massive scale of the anonymous crowd.[2]

Eliot gives us a place the presence of which is cold, forbidding, and purely functional, one that is indifferent to its denizens' dreams and aspirations, supplying their needs in a process of supply and demand built on a nexus of cash and commodity. This is so even where their emotional lives are concerned, as in perfunctory daytime sex—for example, the girl who looks at herself in the mirror with despondency, left alone after her midday tryst.[3]

The central canonical works of British Modernism place the urban experience at the heart of the definition of Modernity. Their interest is often in terms of how cities demolish the geography of belonging: a city in their exploration has no neighborhood, no patterns of relationships founded on time and tradition. As the city has to function via transitory, ephemeral connections between people, often in their social and professional roles, so the sensitive artist at the center is a victim, representative of this "ache of modernity," as Hardy called it.

These notions are perhaps most clearly seen in James Joyce's *Dubliners* (1904). Here, Joyce's stated "moral paralysis" threaded through the stories is a metaphor for the enervating effects of the opposite of Eliot's city. The Dubliners are trapped, enmeshed in a paradoxical city—one with neighborhood, with society and belonging, but ultimately dissatisfying to the artist. In these stories, Joyce is writing about that paradox: that a city in Ireland, a nation essentially rural and small-scale, is restricted by religious and moral dogma in the microcosm of the stories. But it goes deeper: the rottenness of the physical bodies of people suggests degeneration; their concerns are often so narrow and trivial that the protagonists are marginalized by these forces. One of the most informative in this context is "A Little Cloud," a story in which a young aspiring poet meets his friend, Gallaher, who has "made it" as a writer in England. Chandler, in dreaming about his own success as a poet, dreams and considers his "Irishness" as part of his success in England:

He began to invent sentences and phrases from the notice which his book would get. "Mr. Chandler has the gift of easy and graceful verse." . . . "A wistful sadness pervades these poems." . . . "The Celtic note." It was a pity his name was not more Irish-looking. Perhaps it would be better to insert his mother's name before the surname: Thomas Malone Chandler.[4]

Joyce repeats the persona of the sensitive loner in the city, distanced from the self as well as from the center of things, and the "center," as with Chandler, is usually London, not Dublin. Therefore, Duffy in "A Painful Case" repeats sentences about himself in the third person and cannot make an emotional commitment. When he sees two lovers in the dark we are made to see at once the anomie generated both by the city but also by the suburb.

The suburb is arguably more relevant than the city in determining how a sense of the regional was evoked in this period. The suburb and the southern county as concepts were beginning to coalesce, as the railways took people quickly into such areas as the Chilterns or the South Downs. Here, Georgian poetry comes to represent a shift in the sense of region from one circumscribed by established tradition (Wessex, Potteries, Lowlands, etc.) to one, though named and described, which came to be emblematic of a wider concern: that of renewal.

Edward Thomas found forces for renewal in the naming and description of England and Wales, and his intensifying evocation of the rural counties begins to open up the whole subject of borders. Just as a suburb had become a borderland, so a journey into an English region became, in Thomas's hands, an invitation to redefine belonging. His most anthologized poem, "Adlestrop," is quintessentially this statement of being in a borderland removed from modernity. In the quiet rural station the narrator of the poem imagines a place untouched and forgotten, but with a quiescent energy waiting to be called on:

> And for that minute a blackbird sang
> close by, and round him, mistier,
> farther and farther, all the birds
> of Oxfordshire and Gloucestershire.[5]

Thomas imagines a place in which the machine stops, the modern has to contemplate, against its will, that which is eternal, horizonless, beyond truly defining. The vista contains a dream of regions, shires unchanged by the iron rails and by the travelers stuck there for a few minutes.

Thomas's England is symbolic of that land of home created in mythic childhood, and it reminds us that regional belonging and the invention of regional affinity is a narrative of longing, of being natural in a place, and it is expressed better in non-English words, such as the Welsh *hiraeth* or the German–Jewish *Heimlich*. The English word "homely" reaches out into other connotations, irrelevant to the idea. In Thomas's poem "Lob," for instance, what begins in "hawthorn-time in Wiltshire" develops into an affirmation of the quintessential Englishman—a rural being:

> He is English as this gate, these flowers, this mire,
> and when at eight years old Lob-lie-by-the-fire
> came in my books, this was the man I saw,
> he has been in England long as dove and daw.[6]

In this first decade of the twentieth century, a number of prose works and the poetry of the Georgians in particular detailed the mythic figures of Englishman Hodge, the Celt, the countryman, and the peasant worker as somehow representative of a vanishing microcosm. The huge complex macrocosmic cities and their spreading, invidious conurbations were placing an increasing number of Britons in a suburb in which their borderland was becoming a zone of alienation. This alienation was seen as a state detached from a naturally circumscribed life of relationships, home, and stability. The condition of these figures of wise simplicity were visited and textualized, invented as part of a metanarrative of Britain in such diverse forms as Synge's west of Ireland peasants, Thomas's English country people, and Lawrence's Brangwens of Nottinghamshire. But there was also the worm in the apple: there was the dark side of this microcosm, a fabric of a known community that brought with it a penalty in human terms, and in three notable fictional works of this period—James Joyce's *Dubliners* (1904), Caradoc Evans's *My People* (1915), and George Douglas Brown's *The House with the Green Shutters* (1901)—we have an acid criticism of the regional belonging that generates sentiment and distortion. These all deal with Celtic cultures and related to earlier constructions of the fabled Celt as mythic figure; but England had its critic too, with D. H. Lawrence's onslaught on the advance of "ugliness" coming with the spread of industry and the encroachment of a force against the spiritual nourishment of man's instinctual life on the land.

Joyce's *Dubliners* represents the clearest example of the provincial mind and the attitudes of the cultural periphery, but often the issue was linguistic. A prominent role was given in the Modernist period to language, and when Joyce's Gabriel Conroy in "The Dead" spurns the Gaelic League and Miss Ivors at the dinner, he is voicing something at odds with the regional enterprise in writing, in this case in the guise of nationalism. Cultural nationalism in the Celtic–British areas adds a certain depth to the general inquiry about how regions are imagined and invented. Examples abound in the first decades of the twentieth century, but Synge and Hugh MacDiarmid are perhaps the most markedly important advocates of making regional consciousness or national identity a creation of that specific ambiguity in bilingualism. Of course, dialect has always been an element in regional writing, and in, for instance, D. H. Lawrence's fiction it becomes an integral part of his fashioning of local identity. But in the work of Synge and MacDiarmid it becomes the focus of aesthetic interest.

A closer look at the immensely influential works listed above will introduce several concepts into the discussion and locate the sites of dissent and debate about regional writing still prevalent today. What all the works discussed—Synge's *The Playboy of the Western World* (performed 1907), Brown's *The House with the Green Shutters* (1901), and Caradoc Evans's *My People* (1915)—have in common is an ambivalence regarding the subject matter. Synge presents a controversial subject and goes to extremes in terms of poeticized, lyrical rhythms of speech; Evans overtly exploits the language of his Cardiganshire country people as part of his attack; and Brown equally uses his stylistic devices to great ironical effect for those readers fresh from the Kailyard authors.

J. M. SYNGE:
THE PLAYBOY OF THE WESTERN WORLD

It is not the concern of this study to deal with the background of Irish nationalism and the emergence of the Irish Literary Renaissance, but Synge's play is such a rare examination of the regional literary excursion into the well-worn subject of "the peasantry" or "the folk" that its ambiguities need to be summarized. To do this, the social and artistic context has to be given. The Abbey Theatre was opened in 1904, after being initiated as the Irish Literary Theatre in 1899. To further the partly political aims of Yeats's work and the wider cultural nationalism of his colleagues, as T. R. Henn has noted, Synge was recruited as a writer for the cause, but: "Synge's work is non-political, detached, ironic; concerned with this excited yet dispassionate exploration of the world of the western peasantry, and of an imagination that was still 'fiery, magnificent and tender.'"[7]

In contrast, Yeats and others were accessing and retelling a folk inheritance similar to that in Germany a century earlier, when *Das Volk* was a concept indicative of a nonliterary, less sophisticated artistry with a strong appeal of its own. A similar trend was in progress throughout Britain in the years between 1890 and 1930, but there is an immense difference between, say, Georgian lyrics and Synge's lyrical account of a whole Irish regional condition.

In his preface to the play, Synge immediately pinpoints the source of discussion: it is about the degree of realism given in the language of the Mayo fisher people. One driving force of the Irish Literary Revival had been to put on stage a vibrant narrative that was different from the "philistine" realism of the English stage, with its drawing rooms and professional people in minor crisis. In other words, it was to be a drama with an iconoclastic aim as well as a desire to give an authentic view of the people of Ireland. Synge, who had been interested in Celtic identity and history since his days in Paris and who had won a prize at Trinity College for Irish, is at pains in his preface to link literary forebears with current speech. He says: "When the Elizabethan dramatist took his ink-horn and sat down to work he used many phrases he had just heard."[8] He then relates this to his own experience of colloquial conversation over-heard through a floorboard. But he is insistent that the language of his play is naturalistic: "Anyone who has lived in real intimacy with the Irish peasantry will know that the wildest sayings and ideas in this play are tame indeed."[9]

The play brings out again the same issue Hardy faced in his novels: the conviction given the reader that the nonstandard forms of English are authentic and not literary-pastoral. But as produced at the height of Yeats's political drama and of the growth of the Gaelic League, the play was heavily criticized at the time as an insulting and obscene depiction of an aspect of the western Irish character that had previously been tamely depicted, along with a generalized Irish intonation (as in Carle-ton's work, for instance). As the central story-line of the play concerns a young man who brags about his supposed parricide and then wins admiration from the local females, it is a controversial topic to be expressed in "folk poetry" or the supposed heightened natural rhetoric of a country people beyond the pale of sophisticated Dublin salon or club talk.

For instance, the protagonist, Christy, gradually turns from being a shifty, fearful runaway and builds into a poet. Synge, in giving Christy the highly inventive, rhetorical, and richly rhythmical speech of a public poet, lifts the mundane into the mythical:

Christy [grimly]:   It's well you know what call I have. It's well you know it's a lonesome thing to be passing small towns with the lights shining sideways when the night is down, or going in strange places with a dog noising before you . . . or drawn to the cities where you'd hear a voice kissing and talking deep love in every shadow.[10]

Synge is working hard to make the speech he has heard around him in Mayo or Aran seem natural, but it has the unmistakable feel of the artificial, as well constructed as an Augustan parallelism manufactured by Johnson or Swift. This may or may not be unfair, but it typifies the problem of the regional writer in attempting to give his subject to the audience with integrity and directness.

In his metaphors the language is more convincing, as it is rooted in common referents such as "and following after me like an old weasel tracing a rat"; the overall effect is one in which the irony Synge wants to achieve at the closure is increased by the level of complexity in the "peasant" talk. Michael's words on gaining Pegeen Mike's hand are totally convincing as both poetic language and as authentic colloquial talk, as in "but I'm a decent man of Ireland, and I liefer face the grave untimely and I seeing a score of grandsons growing up little gallant swearers . . . than go peopling my bedside with puny weeds."[11]

The wider context of this attempt to give authenticity to a region's speech is in terms of "Kiltartanese," which tends to be stilted and transparently affected. But, as T. R. Henn has pointed out, Synge was dealing with something quite subtle in the speech habits of his subjects: "This Anglo–Irish, based upon the Gaelic structure, echoing its syntax and above all its *tourneurs de phrases*, was spoken by the peasants . . . with a certain hesitation and precision, a kind of deference to the language."[12]

In other words, Synge knew, after living in the west of Ireland for some considerable time, that there was a mental and even an ideological dimension to the speech around him: something related to the center–periphery axis from which regional consciousness becomes acutely integrated into the sense of invention when a myth is made. Just as the Kailyard writers made their people all echo a Scott–Burns-defined Scots nature *in extremis*, so Synge had to match dramatic power with the rhythms of speech he had absorbed, and these were very different from his own linguistic inheritance, from Dublin, and then from Europe.

GEORGE DOUGLAS BROWN: *THE HOUSE WITH THE GREEN SHUTTERS*

Brown's tragic narrative of small-town hubris and the encroachment of modernity is set within a wider version of displacement: that increasingly strident element in regional writing which deals with notions of the center and periphery with a recognition of the mind-set of the provincial. Here, the terms "provincial" and "regional" overlap. In the novel, Brown creates a whole collection of oppositions, with the binaries of rural and urban, simple and sophisticated, emotional and intellectual at the center.

The place itself—Barbie—suggests "barbative," and from the beginning, as we see Gourlay through the eyes of elders and the focal moral channeling of the deacon, we are positioned in such a way that we sense the provincial narrowness familiar from much Victorian fiction. But as the strands of business against emotional motivations expand, there is a sharp sense of fearful foreboding as the young Gourlay goes to college in Edinburgh and his father is victimized by business rivals. The discussion of the railway company and the mention of temporary housing for workers contrasts powerfully with the lyrical accounts of the place itself and its fundamental wild beauty. Brown often gives this beauty with the pointed contrast of the man-made presence:

The brake swung on through merry cornfields where reapers were at work, past happy brooks flashing to the sun, through the solemn hush of ancient and mysterious woods, beneath the great white-moving clouds and blue spaces of the sky. And amid the suave enveloping greatness of the world, the human pismires stung each other and were cruel, full of hate and malice and petty rage.[13]

The novel is fundamentally concerned with the ideology of possession; it deals with home, land, encroachment, and trespass. But Brown, despite his aim of showing the Scottish country-dwellers as anything but sentimental and the opposite of Kailyard denizens, does steal into the narrative some specific insights about "small-town" and sophisticated metropolitan consciousness that became much larger issues in the work of the Northern novelists of the 1960s. For instance, his psychology of young John Gourlay, after winning the Raeburn essay prize at university, is used expertly to develop the theme of that particular act of despising home from a standpoint of intellectual bohemianism familiar with, for instance, Joyce.

Brown spells this out, clarifying the changes of attitude to regional belonging when the perception of the periphery becomes tainted with the sophisticated self-creation of the adolescent:

To go farther, and get the length of Edinburgh, was dangerous, because you came back with a halo of glory around your head which banded your fellows together in a common attack on your pretensions. It was his lack of pretension to travel, however, that banded them against young Gourlay.[14]

Brown very didactically juxtaposes the human and the natural in order to pinpoint these actions by the human "pismires." His assessment of the human animal, as in his Scottish guise, is relentlessly negative and critical. However, in young Gourlay, he is eager to explain the belonging, the pull of place, speaking of Barbie as being defined by a true native as a place full of variety and never bland, whose fields are "not similar as pancakes; they have their differences; each leaps to the eye with a remembered and peculiar charm."[15]

The last third of the novel, being concerned largely with young Gourlay, is where Brown inserts his apologia for the Scottish version of the "homeland" theme in regional invention. He adds this explanation to Gourlay's love of home:

That is why the heart of the Scot dies in flat Southern lands; he lives in a vacancy; at dawn there is no Ben Agray to nod recognition through the mists.[16]

In these first decades of the twentieth century, in the versions of home, belonging, and region across the various categories of region—England, the Celtic nations, county-based narratives, and so on—there is a recurrent interest in the nature of home and place, mostly in terms of challenging the methodology of Victorian encomia and inventions of mythic "folk" identity. Yet, as Brown's novel shows, any attempt to set the native against the foreign, the homely against the distant threat will always entail a retelling of the fundamental literary and cultural definitions of belonging.

In Scotland, this debate on Scottishness, so prominent in Brown and in his response to the Kailyard, is taken up with a much more ambitious cosmopolitan sweep by Hugh MacDiarmid in "A Drunk Man Looks at a Thistle" (1926), discussed in the next chapter. In England, comparisons could be made with the work of D. H. Lawrence, whose most representative regional writing compares well with Brown's fiction. Like Brown, Lawrence is interested in what emerges when we are made to see ourselves from an external stance. His critique of the English fear of the emotions in relational communication is very similar to Brown's critical focus on the life-denying deacon and the "bodies" of Barbie.

In his short stories, Lawrence presents the interweaving subjects of place and home in such ways that he challenges certain versions of Englishness, notably the Puritan inheritance and the work ethic. In "You

Touched Me," for instance, the charity-home boy, Hadrian, comes to live with the sisters Emmie and Matilda. When he comes to manhood, his threat is finally to their instinctive fear of touch, of human closeness. Their Puritan ideology has deeply limited their ability to be spontaneous and to express feelings. Repeatedly, Lawrence tells this as the English malaise, and he sets up regional life as a site for exploring this weakness. When Matilda accidentally touches Hadrian in his bed, Lawrence sums up the repercussions in this way:

She was white and trembling. Suddenly she flushed with anger.
　"It's so indecent," she said.
　"How?" He retorted. "You touched me."[17]

Usually Lawrence is interested in the large-scale historical sweep of land and time, attachments and loss within the regional consciousness, and his main novels (examined in the next chapter) confront the issues of accelerated social change and basic revolutions in the structures of feeling and thinking in modernity. But in many of the short stories he summarizes the notions of place and home more simply. In "Odour of Chrysanthemums," for example, the Midlands colliery and its adjacent human dwellings become a focus for the eternal, elemental truth of death and loss, and in a working-class setting he finds ways of explaining how the Industrial Revolution and the loss of the closeness to nature in English life are apparent in such a traditional ritual as the laying out and washing of the young miner's corpse. Lawrence locates many of the central characteristics of regional consciousness in this changeless, uncomplicated acceptance within the workers: writing in a continuous line of commentary on the dignity of work and the threat of displacement, going from Gaskell, through Hardy, to the innovations of Modernist fiction.

In contrast, Brown's Barbie is a place that is openly threatened from within and without, but it is the innate qualities of the inhabitants that form the core of the novel's exploration of place and identity via Scottish settlement and attitudes to home. Gourlay's *House with the Green Shutters* is "a worthy counterpart to its owner. . . . A house that challenges regard in that way should have a gallant bravery in its look. . . . Gourlay's house was worthy its commanding station. A little dour and blunt in the outlines like Gourlay himself, it drew and satisfied your eye as he did."[18]

CARADOC EVANS: *MY PEOPLE*

Few texts dealing with specific people and communities within Britain can have had such a powerful impact on public feeling as Evans's uncompromising fictional vision of a rural Cardiganshire area and its ideological processes in the minds of people. Published in 1915, it was the work of an aspiring journalist and draper, working in London, away from Wales, and it caused a sensation. As John Harris's edition has made clear, in England the reception of the book was generally high praise, but some thought the language "too stark and austere to be realistic."[19] In Wales, the responses was heated, extreme, and turbulent. Harris explains this with an important point:

The charge that a species of nonconformity is the enemy of the imagination, repressive of art, literature, human feeling and the true welfare of the people, struck all the more deeply for being aimed at the Welsh heartland by one of its number. From such areas had sprung the Liberal-nonconformist leadership, an establishment which encouraged the view of *y werin* (the common people) as an unblemished repository of God-given talent.[20]

Here was a collection of short stories, based on the moral and religious attitudes of a community in Cardiganshire, Rhydlewis in the Ceri valley, which depicted the human relationships of the chapel-going elders as ruthless, uncompromising, and based largely upon a cash nexus and a relentless ideology of gain and condemnation. This is even more stunning when the historical context is summarized. As Harris noted, from the last decades of the nineteenth century, the mythic narrative of *y werin* had been consolidated, and a Wales of the mind had been created through wide cultural dissemination and the consolidation of the *Eisteddfod* traditions. In 1866 Cymru Fydd (Young Wales) had been formed in London with an agenda of campaigns for disestablishment; the Cymmrodorion group, from 1873, had moved into its most potent phase of activity, including having an impact on Welsh education, and the general literary construction of Wales was very much as exemplified by Edward Thomas's book, *Wales* (1905), in which the tradition of Borrow is taken up and extended.

It is hard to reconcile Thomas's Wales with Caradoc Evans's homeland. The religious foundation of all diurnal duties and roles, together with the underpinning notions of regulated life and behavior, is, for Evans, a terribly repressive and inflexible social force. His character

Twm Tybach, the irreligious poacher and outcast in "The Glory That Was Sion's," is dying, and the people discuss his burial: is he fit for burial in the traditional graveyard, or in a new one? The leader of the congregation visits Twm, and Evans gives us a typical textualization of this powerful local figure. He is made a poetic, rhetorical figure of great presence, and Twm is pathetically small. In Evans, the preachers and religious figures are written into the stories as awesome in their convictions, and the place is as hard as the Biblical language Evans uses. But Thomas, in writing about rural Wales and the chapel, heightens matters:

And there is Siloh at—, standing bravely,—at night, it often seems perilously, at the end of a road, beyond which rise immense mountains and impassable, and in my memory, always the night and a little, high, lonely moon, haunted forever by a pale grey circle. . . . But Siloh stands firm, and ventures once a week to send up a thin music that avails nothing against the wind.[21]

Thomas gives us bards and schoolmasters, mountains and innkeepers; his Wales is still the picturesque of Tintern prints and Borrow's wanderings. The above, written in 1905, gives an account of what Evans purposely wanted to challenge. His rural community is ruled by marriage negotiations, repression of emotion, unthinking allegiance to Biblical rulings, and a basic lack of full interaction between people: everything is done through roles, expected attitudes, and bargains struck.

Evans's Cardiganshire is a region defined by language again. As Joyce, Synge, and Lawrence, so Evans creates a specific blend of literary intonations and rhythms to set against the colloquial speech. *My People* is related by this means, and the result is the foregrounding of local language assembled by means of dialectal grammar, vocabulary, and, mostly, terms of address or relational denotation, as when he uses Welsh terms such as "bach" or "the Big Man" for God within the fabric of discourse. A typical example is in the story "The Way of the Earth," in which Jenkins, a tradesman, courts Sara for her dowry. In the negotiations with her father, we have:

"Shall we take up this business then at once?" Mishtir Jenkins observed.
  "Make plain Sara Jane's inheritance."
  "Much, little boy."
  "Penrhos will come to Sarah Jane then?"

"Iss, man."

"Right that is then, Simon, wealthy am I. Do I not own Shop General? Man bach, there's a grand business for you!"[22]

Evans gives this minimal, reductive speech alongside the rhetorical of the Biblical rhythms, and the result is a syntax in which pulses of phrases and hard consonantal sounds assault the sense of the personal and the human interaction.

These various writings of Joyce, Synge, Brown, and Evans suggest the sheer range of contexts involved in exploring the regional consciousness in these years. Within Modernist writing generally, displacement was emerging as a focal idea, so it comes as no surprise that writers with a variety of backgrounds used their cultural inheritance as a basis for both criticism of accepted narrative norms and the challenge to the dominance of the local and provincial in British writing before the growth of the metropolis.

What they have in common is the fascination with the new urban experience and how this relates to conventional writing in English about stability and permanence, tradition and common experience. In a world in which both shared experience and known communities were becoming rare, writers were coping with the evolution of a new regional and national awareness. Identity was now often national, of course, in the burgeoning nationalist movements in Ireland and Scotland, and the perception of a Celtic renaissance in the writings of Yeats, Joyce, Brown, MacDiarmid, and Synge seems more ambitious, wide-framed, and eclectic than the Welsh variety of regional writing. Evans's stories show a rural Wales entrapped in its own fabric of possession: the new versions of Welshness, perhaps influenced by the fact of so much English and Irish settlement for the industries of South Wales, were becoming bifurcated as "Gogs" and "Taffs" were given differing positions as literary subjects. That is to say, the Welsh literary inheritance, like the Scottish, was particularly bookish, scholarly, and narrow. But where Scotland had had Burns and Scott to create regional identity on a mythic scale, Wales had only just opened up Anglo–Welsh literary possibilities at the time Evans was published.

Overall, then, the Modernist period saw region and province as terms related to the problematic of displacement: as the metropolis became the center of avant-garde art and the cities attracted young writers toward a new mode of being, so regional narrative and poetry became potentially retrograde, either following the dialect poets, such as William Barnes in Dorset or the Yorkshire almanacs, or producing mass-market fiction, such as the work of Eden Philpotts or Hugh Walpole. English regions were becoming quaint rural backwaters for oral history and folk song, and the Celtic areas were emerging as vibrant, multifaceted sites of innovative writing. The result was that by the 1920s, with MacDiarmid and Neil Gunn, for instance, or with Priestley in Yorkshire, the trend was swinging back to contrary voices, often of individualists, insisting that regional belonging was still a productive, highly creative force in modern writing.

By the time documentary and film arrived as potent forces to influence narratives of displacement, a rediscovery of regional awareness was in process; but old patterns of thought die hard, and all aspects of the subject were to be massively affected by the cultural industries of the 1930s. The theme of England and Englishness, so prominent in the interwar years, was linked to the nature of local allegiance, and D. H. Lawrence stands as a hugely influential figure here. In one of his last works—the essay, "Nottingham and the Mining Country" (written in 1929, a year before his death)—he introduces a critical note that has been taken up by most major writers since then: the paradox of attraction and revulsion in what is small-scale, neglected, unattractive, and notably against a cosmopolitan frame of mind. His reflections on his father's mining community provokes this criticism:

The real tragedy of England, as I see it, is the tragedy of ugliness. The country is so lovely: the man-made England is so vile. . . . In my father's generation, with the old wild England behind them, and the lack of education, the man was not beaten down, what with the din-din-dinning of Board schools, books, cinemas, clergymen, the whole national and human consciousness hammering on the fact of material prosperity above all things.[23]

Here, Lawrence locates that specific interest in the regional consciousness: an antipathy to the center, to change, and to authority. The challenge from uniformity and the relentless force of centralization effected by industrial and commercial change, he argues, created a certain ugliness, and this shifted from a noun referring to landscape to an inner human defect—an inability to live by instinct. Hardy had seen the same threat in *Tess of the D'Urbervilles*: the "ache" of modernity, in her case coming from the impact of the educational system and the encroachment of change and mechanization. For both Lawrence and Hardy, what had been lost in human terms was almost always related to the ideas of belonging and community at the heart of the British experience: a basically agrarian set of states with geographical varieties so extreme and historical factors so complex that regional writers had a special place. It was up to them to tell the story—or invent another story— explaining the loss of belonging and the nature of displacement. If the twentieth century was to be characterized by shifting populations, deracination by war, and emigration through political intolerance, then perhaps all these things were rooted in the desire to change the character of place, area, region, and, finally, nation?

Regional writing from around 1920 became a literary element that had to cope with more than the advent of the railways or the first cities: it was now a case of radical changes in demography initiating new ways of seeing: fresh perceptions of what home means and what it had once meant. The documentary movement was to be a prominent factor here, as German idealism (an influence on John Grierson) impinged on a range of philosophies about identity. These idealistic modes of being were to be seen in people working, and work was to become a means of understanding what regional belonging was all about.

6

Displacement to Documentary

Between D. H. Lawrence's *Sons and Lovers* (1913) and the emergence of "proletarian literature" in the 1930s, the notion of regional belonging was transmuted into something attached to new explorations of work, automation, and the self. Writing with very different objectives, the generation of regional writers on the scene at the time of the First World War and through to the 1930s had to confront massive forces of centralization and uniformity. At around the same time when Synge and Evans were giving their interpretations of microcosmic communities, others were attempting to relate issues of national and regional identity to grander philosophical schemes of thought. The diversity is on a major scale—everything from Hugh MacDiarmid's meditations on Scottishness to Lawrence's increasing criticism of his native Nottinghamshire within the wider frame of social change as materialism advanced.

The focus shifted from the mechanisms of insularity and known community to themes of asking why and in what ways regional writing still mattered. During the years of the First World War, Lawrence's critique of Britain was partly based on his perceptions of the values and nature of a community seen as a series of bonds and duties, working by trust and mutual help. He always maintained that the "intimacy" of miners below ground was something special and that their separate male world, revolving around pub culture, sport, and nature, was somehow integral to the land and to the processes of natural cyclical change—that they were bound to the place as much as to the community. In *The Rainbow* (1915), Lawrence is interested in the impact of modern consciousness on the patterns of life embedded in farming, the land, and the family. The Brangwens encounter modernity in the form of a European consciousness just as much as in the new sensibility of the governing class of the nouveaux riches. But in all his work there is a continuing interest in the formation of self-knowledge and sense of identity through place.

In *Sons and Lovers* we have a sustained account of this mode, in which Lawrence has to explain the mining community and Mr. Morel, as if examining how they came to be such a separate case study of belonging, with all its limitations and shortcomings. Still the use of dialect persists as a defining method: a partly realistic but partly lyrical impulse to explain regional difference through the most specific instrument of self-authentication in existential terms—the native tongue. In Hugh MacDiarmid's long philosophical poem, "A Drunk Man Looks at a Thistle" (1926), this language of instinctual being is a source of MacDiarmid's journey through Scottishness and its voicing of belonging. What emerges here is one of the dominant preoccupations of regional and national writing—duality:

> A man's a clean contrairy sicht
> turned this way in-ootside,
> and, fegs, I feel like Dr. Jekyll
> tak'n a guid tent o' Mr. Hyde.[1]

and, later:

> Or use o'England whaur the UK's meent,
> or this or that, anent the Blue Saltire,
> recruitin', pedigrees, and Gude kens what,
> filled wi' a proper patriotic fire."[2]

Again, as with Synge, MacDiarmid is mixing bookish, dictionary Scots with his own Scots, natural to him; in what Alan Bold has called "names for nameless things," MacDiarmid was working hard to counteract the kind of Scots established as a "homemade product cultivated in the kailyard and handled by amateurs."[3] In doing this, he had to work hard for a naturalness based on dramatized personae in which to project the vernacular language and culture.

This example also explains Lawrence's dilemma: his stance, when successful and lionized by London literary people, as a "regional novelist," with only his home county to write about. Before we had Lawrence the traveler and citizen of the world, we had a dialect speaker—in effect, a bilingual writer like MacDiarmid. Where the man C. M. Grieve created the poet MacDiarmid, Lawrence the miner's son made Lawrence the English writer, at home among those at Garsington and in the London salons.

As the twentieth century wore on, this duality in the regional awareness of several important writers became a fusion of natural and acquired knowledge and culture. In *Sons and Lovers*, Lawrence, although arguably primarily interested in mother–son affections and the awakening of the sexual being, uses the father character, Walter Morel, as an *exemplum*, a pattern of the man attached to place, circumscribed by the patterns of life and nature he was born into. This particular version of the "blinkered provincial" is radically different from, say, Bennett's workers or businessmen of the Potteries. In Lawrence, they are organic with everything in their diurnal being: he gives them to the reader through their dialect, injecting their dilemma in the face of change and the threat of the modern with dialectal precision from the very beginning, when Walter courts his wife-to-be:

"And you are a miner!" she exclaimed in surprise.
"Yes, I went down when I was ten."
She looked at him in wondering dismay.
"When you were ten! And wasn't it very hard?" she asked.
"You soon get used to it. You live like th' mice, and you pop out at night to see what's going on."
"It makes me feel blind," she frowned.
"Like a mouldiwarp!" he laughed, "Yi, an' there's some chaps as does go round like mouldiwarps." He thrust his face forward in the blind, snout-like way of a mole."[4]

In this entire conversation, Walter gradually changes from a careful, hesitant speech to the natural fluency of his self-expression, in dialect. In the first half of the novel, as Walter develops from the mild, humorous miner into the tyrant, Lawrence is orchestrating the elements of dissension and challenge inherent in the individual's move from self-preoccupation to social being. In his dialect, Walter is locked into the earth as into himself. The challenge of life through sexuality, courtship, marriage, and fatherhood combines to present him with a complex of demands that is too much for his low-key selfhood.

Lawrence repeatedly says that Walter had "denied the God in him" and so lost all communication with his family, and he implies also a loss as he experiences this emergence, this evolutionary change. Paul Morel, in contrast, is made to voice the Lawrentian spirit in the face of that modernity which created the modern materialistic mode of being:

Then he looked wistfully out of the window. Already he was a prisoner of industrialism. Large sunflowers stared over the old red wall of the garden opposite, looking in their jolly way down on women who were hurrying with something for dinner. The valley was full of corn, brightening in the sun. Two collieries, among the fields, waved their small white plumes of steam. Far off on the hills were the woods of Annesley, dark and fascinating. Already his heart went down. He was being taken into bondage.[5]

This is typical of many elements in Lawrence's work in which the man-made industrial landscape is ambiguous in its presence. The woods are a mystery, but the colliery is transparent in its functioning; it is now an integral part of the landscape, yet it has forced on Paul's father and the other miners a kind of relational nexus at once sensuous and unnatural. Paul, like most of Lawrence's protagonists who take on a persona nature, longs for an immersion in the mystery; he wants the fear in the dark woods. That unknown has to be also in himself—hence the sexuality in his love for Miriam and, indeed, his mother-attachment involves an end to the separate, demarcated ground of his father and the world of men.

Yet Lawrence's world of the working man is also a precursor of the working man of documentary fiction, and little has been written on the progression from Lawrence to, for instance, Stan Barstow or George Orwell. It is easy to assume that Lawrence's miners are merely splinters from the edifice of ideas within his fictional and didactic framing of his narratives of awakening and loss. But that variety of regional belonging in the worker in the modern industrial and commercial society in Lawrence's work mirrors the alienation of the worker, set against the pride of work and craft so prominent in the Englishness of rural writers from Jefferies to Flora Thompson.

A summary of how Lawrence depicts his working men in the Midland mining counties provides a switch of representation from the intimacy of miners below ground to the brooding, resentful, aggressive dark miners at the gate outside the Crich domain in *Women in Love*. In this context, it has to be stressed that the gamekeeper, Mellors, in *Lady Chatterley's Lover* (1928) arguably represents a quintessence of this integral relationship of man with land and "blood-relation" that Lawrence derived from his observation of the miners' lives and attitudes.

Lawrence's progression from presenting the mining community as an Arcadia, a male idyll where work and games and brotherhood create a central factor in the regional consciousness, to the restless mob of *Women in Love* is a radical change, reflecting the growing unease about regional belonging as partly a pastoral vision:

Seething mobs of men marched about, their faces lighted up as for holy war, with a smoke of cupidity. How disentangle the passion for equality from the passion for cupidity, when begins the fight for equality of possessions? But the God was the machine.[6]

This gives the polar opposite to:

The collier went to the pub and drank in order to continue his intimacy with his mates. They talked endlessly, but it was rather of wonders and marvels, even in politics, than of facts. . . . He loved the countryside, just the indiscriminating feel of it.[7]

This is much closer to the kind of community engendered by place and regional difference in, for instance, *Tess of the D'Urbervilles* than anything close to the twentieth-century malaise of displacement.

Lawrence is attracted to the theme of displacement in a sense of land and tradition, love and belonging. MacDiarmid is close to this, but he is primarily in the nationalistic urge to be differentiated—by speech as much as by historical perspective and awareness. Starting their writing careers at about the same time, they illustrate the diversity of representation initiated by the impulse to write with a regional perspective, be that a nationalist concept or an ideological one. But Lawrence's workers are also formed by community, or even made or broken by the nature of the immediate community, and if that sense of workful purpose is broken, then communal feeling disintegrates.

Displacement in the context of the regional perspective is thus a factor in the effects of the Modernist imperative. But it should be recalled that the early documentarists, such as Grierson, on film, and the early 1930s writers, such as Orwell (notably in *Keep the Aspidistra Flying* and *Coming Up for Air*), had a great deal to say about the pull of home and community, and they had behind them the notion of idealism. This philosophical line of thought led to the view that in his working self, for instance, an ideal perception of man could be made through aesthetic vision. Thus, as in the Victorian images of muscular navigators or builders we have man in some ideal form of activity, so in regional writing we have the perfect site of appropriation for this to become a defining instrument of belonging and "natural" being. Hence, Grierson's fishermen in his documentary film, *Drifters* (1929), simultaneously showed people in their working environment with convincing naturalistic imagery and in such a way that the viewer is observing work via *homo faber*: the narrative of the film creates a harmony between worker, task, and place as integrated and cohesive as that of the early visions of the regional in, for instance, Wordsworth or Scott. As Valentine Cunningham has commented: "No wonder literary men wanted to become camera-men"[8] after such imagistic narratives of ideal work.

It would be no exaggeration to say that the renewed interest in British regions in the interwar years was predominantly related to the first truly educative crusade to find "England" or "Britain" in its diversity rather than in its status as a political power with a fading empire. There are many reasons for the acceleration of the documentary method in these years: the boom in travel writing abroad, which meant that people turned their attention to more distant parts of Britain, the crisis in poverty and deprivation in the regions, a widespread interest in didactic fiction, and a fascination with the class system in the context of the rise of socialism.

One writer in these years who certainly had a powerful influence on the nature of regional writing was J. B. Priestley. His *English Journey*, based on a trip made in 1933, confirms the general appraisal of Priestley as a Yorkshire writer, but also as a writer who is deeply interested in the questions of local identity and its social and historical causes. His fiction was often set in Yorkshire, and his reportage in this book shows his novelist's eye for detail; the most telling episode is in his long reflections on his home city, Bradford. Priestley is at his best when explaining and describing community, sharing, and human warmth; he is a writer about society who prefers the celebration of friendship above abstract speculation. His common sense and his acuity in matters of relationships and structures of belonging create a sense of wonder as well as of practical, everyday matters.

Priestley's account of the Bradford of 1933 says a great deal about that persistent motif of regional writing: the elegiac tone and the stimulus to memory and imagination given by a known community. Priestley sums up his feelings like this:

I have changed of course; but I think the place itself has changed more than I have. And I am not thinking now of those inevitable alterations in the appearance of a large town; the new streets where once there were old pubs and shops; the miles of semi-detached villas where once I rolled among the gigantic buttercups and daisies. These changes are more significant. A sight of them here may give a glimpse of two Englands, two worlds.[9]

The "two Englands" are, repeatedly throughout the book, the past and the present, the urban and the rural, but he makes a point of demonstrating how industrialization removed the essentially medieval England of the shires, with distances perceived before the railways and the internal combustion engine. This is the focal quest of the documentary era, when places were being revisited to gauge to what extent the myth of historical invention of the British regions had been eroded. For example, when Priestley visits Chipping Campden, he makes the point that "The whole of this region, though it seems Arcadian, is actually a depressed industrial area,"[10] and he stresses that, contrary to popular belief about the Cotswolds, "Even as late as 1801 a map of England showing the density of population includes this region in its most heavily shaded areas."[11]

Regional writing has always been based on the understood differentiation of peoples across the land, and the diversity, racial and sociological, throughout time, of settlements and communities. From around 1930 to the Northern novel of the 1960s, there was a profound need to celebrate and acknowledge these differences. As Phyllis Bentley wrote in an essay in 1941: "Paradoxical as a diverse England sounds, that paradox is true. It will be well first to investigate this diversity, since it is the *fons et origo* of English regional literature."[12]

Documentary is a style as well as a genre, of course, and it has to be stressed that in the 1930s there was an intense interest in both, largely because of political and ideological agendas. It was an age of manifestos and of the committed individual artist. Fashionable leftist stances led to the concept of "proletarian literature," and this was inextricably linked with regional writing. As the various aesthetic standpoints were worked out, one factor in the literary scene became clear: Britain had its working class and descendants of the "peasantry," as conventionally termed. Why not go and find these, just as had happened in other countries? Maxim Gorky in Russia, and the new naturalistic novelists in France, the heirs of Zola, had done something similar. Film had also led the way.

One group that typifies this attitude was the editorial panel behind the magazine, *Fact*, as discussed in the introduction; but there was also the influential *Penguin New Writing*, edited by John Lehmann. He included sections of documentary under various names, such as "Report on Today," "The Way We Live Now," and "The Living Moment." These pieces were often accounts of work or places. The spirit was very much exploratory of an unknown or foolishly neglected England—the country where menial tasks were done and in which traditional patterns of life were still to be observed at the periphery of cultural reference. Many of the notable writers of the 1930s and 1940s included a heavily factual documentary element. The qualities desired were listed by Arthur Calder-Marshall in his survey of the contents of the *Fact* special issue. He refers to the "realistic" and "reflective" novel, and Calder-Marshall insists that the new demand is for a vibrancy unseen in the works of middle-class writers. He writes:

Modern education and newspapers have made the middle classes articulate in the sense that they have set phrases coined ready for the set situations that occur to them: but this very glibness has at the same time destroyed the originality that less articulate workers strike in the labour of thought.[13]

He wants writers to abandon the liberal attitudes of their predecessors and the focus of the onslaught is class, not place, but the logical consequence of such thinking is that the supposed "natural writers and speakers" are found on the cultural periphery—on the land, in factories, down the mines, and so on. Hence, the November issue of *Fact* is on a South Wales mining town, and one major interest is in the nature of the communal sense and the energy in the people in spite of poverty and unemployment.

This documentary–regional literature is also based on the need to understand the depth of Britain's resources, but the constant urge to look and listen in places that have previously been neglected or misrepresented is always there. It can take the form of a lyrical and elegiac view of England past and present, as in George Orwell's *Coming Up for Air* (1939); it can be sinewy and direct life-writing, such as B. L. Coombes's *Miner's Day* (1945); or it may be a finely structured account of the complexities of regional life, as in Winifred Holtby's *South Riding* (1936).

Orwell's hero, George Bowling, at the moment of personal and, indeed, world political crisis, returns to his home village and looks for some element of stability amid the chaos of imminent war and the potential destruction of everything that defines his England. Orwell, in including factual and didactic strains in his work (such as the lengthy account of hop-picking in Kent in *A Clergyman's Daughter*), was eager to counteract such attitudes as the ones displayed by the *Fact* editors, and—as he said in an essay written in 1943—left-wing literary criticism had not been wrong to insist on the need to make subject-matter central, nor to ask for a propaganda element. But "where it has been wrong is in making what are ostensibly literary judgements for political ends."[14] For this reason, what Orwell does in *Coming Up for Air* is make the idyllic dream of the distant, peripheral rural location symbolic of some inner spirit of Englishness.

Orwell makes the focus for this a pool in which Bowling fished as a boy. The place is Lower Binfield—a place where on market day "Chaps with round red faces like pumpkins and dirty smocks and huge boots covered in cow-dung . . . used to drive their brutes to the market-place."[15] Orwell also explains why fishing is an ideal metaphorical means of defining this England of the mind:

As soon as you think of fishing you think of things that don't belong to the modern world. The very idea of sitting all day under a willow tree beside a quiet pool . . . belongs to the time before the war, before the radio, before Hitler. There's a kind of peacefulness even in the names of English coarse fish. Roach, rudd, dace, bleak, barbel, bream.[16]

Throughout his work, Orwell was profoundly interested in what defined the English and the sense of Englishness; of course, for him it was bound up with class, education, and empire; yet in his fiction he carefully documented the notion of place and rural existence in the English consciousness, deliberately avoiding the sentimental mode but always asserting the depth and power of these abiding images of belonging and identity.

The documentary–regional of these years had to explain life as if for missionaries or aliens. Bert Coombes, a Welsh miner, was published first in John Lehmann's *New Writing*, but in his book *Miner's Day* we have a typical example of this didacticism. It is written very well indeed, integral with the expression of a lifestyle radically different from that of the London readers who had very little idea of life down the mine. In fact, mining literature in the 1930s provides perhaps the clearest instance of the integration of documentary and regional writing. The former was a method, the latter a subject. In *Miner's Day*, Coombes concentrates on the way in which the miners' lives are identified with some of the myths of the countryman but also totally different, as the diurnal round of work and family circumscribes a narrow boundary on them. When the miners spend a morning in Neath, for instance, their attention is on the idea of farming. "They pet the calves, and they appreciate the pigs. . . . Interest in pigs is more understandable." As Crush says, "If I had enough money, like, I might buy a pig—if I had a cot and some grub to give him."[17]

The spirit of this writing, as in the magazines and later in the Mass Observation movement, was to give the minutiae of the routine and also to explain everything, from the general cultural environment to the demands of the work itself. Coombes explains the hard work and the danger in mining, but also such things as Wales on a Sunday : "Even the Welfare Halls are closed . . . save for a stroll along the road in fine weather, or a hill-climb for the more energetic, there is nothing to do or see."[18]

Where this variety of writing genuinely achieves something significant is in the regional works in which an imagined place and people relate to that invention through time and place encountered, for instance, in Blackmore, Hardy, and Barrie. In this period, arguably the most significant achievement is Winifred Holtby's *South Riding*. This is not to deny the importance of Phyllis Bentley and J. B. Priestley in creating a modern Yorkshire firmly within the tradition of imagined Yorkshire. Their works are concerned with historical process, generational conflict, and sheer Yorkshire character. But Holtby's novel manages to incorporate the documentary and the regional in such a way that we have simultaneously something to compare with *Middlemarch* in terms of a provincial study and a narrative with the traits discussed above, facing certain timeless inventions of "Yorkshire-ness."

In the Wedmore Memorial Lecture for 1960, Bentley spoke on "Yorkshire and the Novelist." In her lecture, she convincingly explains the continued interest in Yorkshire as a representative county in the rationale behind regional writing. She describes a dinner for Yorkshire writers in 1938 and points out that in attendance were 182 writers who were eligible because they were "Yorkshire born and bred." She then asks whether there is something special about Yorkshire—the place and the imaginative construct. She notes the diversity of trades throughout the county and historical factors; but it is in the usual indefinable concept of "character" that she finds her real explanation:

> The northern climate, the strong winds blowing in from the North Sea, the Pennine Hills, the distance from the centre of the country's culture, the drop of Danish blood . . . some or all of these factors have combined to produce a character which is . . . sturdy and independent, and at once blunt and reserved.[19]

Bentley notes that *South Riding* is remarkable among Yorkshire texts in that a county council is the hero of a novel, and that the book "sums up in itself the essential temper and type of civilisation of its native county."[20] Bentley knew the basic cultural clash of center and periphery—after her book *Inheritance* was accepted by Gollancz in 1932, she reflected that her clothes were all wrong for London, and in her autobiography she wrote at length on the biographical factors behind her Yorkshire themes.[21] Bentley saw the remarkable achievement of *South Riding* in this respect of showing difference and diversity within a narrative that dealt with essential qualities native to a place and a temperament.

In the novel, Holtby works out her oppositional factors with real skill: the poor of the Shacks and the rich of the baronial halls; local politicians with power and arrogance and people who genuinely want to advance well-being for all and real social progress; the educated who have been "away" and absorbed high culture, and those who have acquired a narrowness of attitude in the distant shire.

Sarah Burton, the new head of Kiplington High School, has been beyond Kingsport and the South Riding, and, as is the case with so many regional novels, Holtby uses her character to provide the essential conflicts and contrasts in the clash of home and abroad and to explore the mind-sets of the parochial as well as the cosmopolitan, much as Brown had done in *The House with the Green Shutters*. But Sarah comes home and through her return Holtby gives us some sharp commentary on this "return" theme of region and belonging. She sees a girl, and then the industrial area, and we are told that "Sarah loved her, loved Kingsport, loved the sailor or fish-porter or whatever man had left upon her the proof of his virility."[22]

More importantly, "after her London life, she had dreaded return to the North lest she should grow slack and stagnant"; and Holtby includes a passage that is representative of how her novel presents and heightens the sense of vitality, the feel of a world quick with life, in the working environment (much as the *Fact* editors wanted to demonstrate such things in language): Sarah is "in love with life and all its varied richness" after seeing a small street of shops: "—not slums, but dreary respectable horrors seething with life which was neither dreary nor respectable."[23] Holtby's novel extends to celebrate individuals with the "character" explained by Bentley, such as the matron at the high school, Miss Parsons: "All over Yorkshire, in farm-houses and shops and villas, lingered the memory of her unstinted service."[24] A prominent technique in the novel is the foregrounding of individuals who represent the dynamic mix of the qualities that present a certain trait of ambiguity in the context of their social world.

But the regional element is seen most strongly in the Holly family, living in the Shacks—deserted railway carriages on the fringe of the community. In the intellectually bright daughter, Lydia, the novel presents perhaps the fundamental theme of the documentary–regional work: the clash of the microcosmic community with the cosmopolitan—the worlds of class-dominated being. Lydia is immersed in the sensual world of the rural poor, similar to the Lawrentian miner's preoccupation with sport, sensuality, and work. Lydia's imperative to "better herself" echoes the long tradition of regional writing stemming from Dorothea Brooke and then Pip in *Great Expectations* through to Paul Morel. The ties of home and the tightly defined world on the edge of the larger social groupings define its inhabitants by duty, role, work-tasks. The call of the macrocosmic world is one of ideals, ambition, transmutation of the self. In Wordsworth's poem, "Michael," we have perhaps the definitive, bold statement about home and abroad as combative elements of destruction and creation, and this theme is stated well there.

In the scene in which Sarah visits Lydia as Lydia's mother is dying, Sarah stays for a very short time and has no idea how ill Mrs. Holly is. Holtby then summarizes Lydia's scholastic tasks and her status at the school just before her mother falls and, shortly afterwards, dies. Juxtaposed, then, are the contexts of home and school, stasis and escape, the mind and the body. Lydia, placed as firmly in her environment as

Hardy's Tess, faces an ordeal, a test, and she learns, grows, in a way beyond book-learning or official character-forming school education. Integral to Lydia's sense of self is the homely landscape, described in such a way that it almost erases the traditional Romantic and elegiac rapture so often given to home community. Holtby gives the reader the visual appeal of the place with "the long green undulating land, netted with dykes like glittering silver wires" but also adds the Wordsworthian coda: "the huge march of the clouds, the tides that ran nearly a mile over the ruddy sand, had become part of her nature."[25] This conflict has always been generic to regional writing. The siren-like call of the macrocosm is irresistible, shadowing the more career-centered professional appeal of the class and status structure of English society. Lydia, like so many protagonists of the British novel since *Jane Eyre* and *David Copperfield*, is nurtured spiritually from a dual source: intellect and spirit. The external, learned behavior of the greater world of ideas offers a version of fulfillment: the spirit is formed and retained by home, community, selfless love. The documentary element in regional writing between Orwell's early work and the work of Sillitoe and Barstow in the 1950s hinged around this duality. Even in Larkin's poetry of the late 1950s, collected in *The Whitsun Weddings* (1960), we have this same duality and ambivalence when the region is contrasted with the metropolitan center. Larkin's travelers from Hull—"the end of England," as he called the city—are given as robustly, coarsely working-class, marrying or seeing marriages (reflecting their own cyclical being, as they quote people who are older relatives) and being "aimed" at London "like an arrow shower."[26] It is as if Larkin is documenting a journey from the regional periphery of selfhood to the center of the married state—individuality and commitment—just as Lydia has to leave her home to be educated and fulfilled. So for Larkin, geography and belonging are inevitably in conflict with the desired fulfillment in escape from the known community of regional consciousness. In Holtby's novel, similarly, the confrontation involves emotional commitment and intellectual ambition.

Consequently, in the regional writing of the twentieth century, after Modernism, the subject of displacement meets its counterpoint in the revisiting of "home" and "belonging" equated with childhood and such character-defining concepts as work, craft, and trade. This is the point at which the notion of self-sufficiency, communal integration, and nature intersect with the documentary. Just as the fiction of the 1930s and 1940s became increasingly concerned with didacticism and with explaining class to class and center to periphery, so the proliferation in life-writing, in the forms of memoir, social history, and autobiographies, provided another route to the understanding of regional consciousness. As discussed in chapter 2, the genre of local communal writing, beginning with Gaskell and Mitford, maintained its status and interest in this period, represented most strikingly by Flora Thompson's book on Oxfordshire life in the late nineteenth century, *Lark Rise to Candleford* (1945).

Thompson writes of a rural community with a barter system, a custom of self-help and cooperation, positively brimming with information and descriptions of trades, skills, and attitudes that in some ways define the nature of existence on the periphery. Thompson refines and interprets the concept of a hamlet: the smallest unit in the geography of English experience. She depicts a world that is premodern, preindustrial, and in fact notably sustained by an oral culture, tradition, and convention.

The simplicity of life in the hamlet is consolidated by the happy ignorance of the sensual, tactile life on the land: "so, for some time, Oxford remained to them a dim blur of bishops. . . . To imagine a place without pigsties and vegetable gardens was more difficult. With no bacon or cabbage, what could people have to eat?"[27]

Thompson presents the idea of regional consciousness as irretrievably attached to the myth of home and domesticity; she provides so much praise for the simple life that the book becomes perhaps the quintessential regional memoir in the category of the known community. Her Oxfordshire, like so many memoirs set in distant, untouched rural Britain, is firmly defined by class, occupation, status, and aspirations. In chapter 16, this is intensified when she describes a previous generation—the mid-Victorians. Here, we could have had the celebration of the microcosm, relating closely to the classical ideal of the *vir bonus*, the "happy man," in rural retreat, all his wants met, but Thompson constantly adds a modern perspective and plays down the idyllic. This is arguably a confrontation with the most persistent generic quality of regional invention: yet this microcosm is represented as the miniature of all the greatest stories, the major themes of human life:

Nothing of outside importance ever happened there and their lives were as unlike as possible the modern conception of country life, for Lark Rise was neither a little hotbed of vice nor a garden of all the Arcadian virtues . . . and many a satisfying little drama was played out on that ten-foot stage.[28]

Lark Rise to Candleford thus equates in some ways to the documentary, didactic modes of the time but also places the virtues of restraint, acceptance, and human relationships at the center of the known community. There is no really revolutionary external element until Laura leaves for a job further afield, and the only strangers are the begging tramps and gypsies.

In much regional writing of this period, there is the recurrence of the motif of the alien, the stranger arriving in the community and thus revealing the essence of the place through an innocent or critical eye. Many writers have made a specific vision of regional belonging clash with a restlessness from within or a stranger from outside; in Scottish writing this is notably important, as the sheer distance and geographical and cultural boundaries between different areas of Scotland have given rise to a vibrant regional literature in the period between about 1920 and 1950. Interesting contrasts may be drawn in this respect between Neil Gunn and Lewis Grassic Gibbon, with Gunn, in *The Key of the Chest* (1945), moved from being what J. B. Pick calls "simply a regional novelist writing about the lives of crofters and fishermen" to a writer profoundly interested in "freedom as fundamental both as an individual drive for discovery and expression, and as an operative principle in society."[29]

With Grassic Gibbon—notably in his trilogy, *A Scots Quair,* written between 1932 and 1934—we have a fiction that advances on the discussion about the use of Scots, following the Kailyard extremes and then Brown's or MacDiarmid's varieties and mixtures of scholarly and colloquial vocabulary and syntax. Gibbon, in an original and quirky style, as Tom Crawford has noted, worked "as if he was writing in English, with only a few modifications. But in reality he achieved something rather different. He cloaked the Scots vocabulary in English spelling, writing 'blether' as 'blither'. . . . But for native speakers, the pronunciations . . . strengthen their conviction that they are participating in a life both familiar and national."[30] So, once more, the prominence of authentic dialect language is at the center of both the stylistic issues and the critical assessments of the degree of success achieved in naturalistic writing.

Gibbon's trilogy centers on Chris Guthrie, a sensitive, independent young woman in the village of Kinraddie. The environs of the community include the sea as well as the mountains, and also the town of Stonehaven, where Chris is educated; Gibbon uses key locations in order to impose recurrent motifs on Chris's story as she becomes a representative figure in that specific version of Scottishness found at the level of the "Kailyard." Gibbon is, however, not only conscious of the presence of Kailyard sentimentalism; he is also aware of the burden placed upon the Scottish writer to deal with the entrenched theme of duality in Scottish writing. The solution, in the trilogy, is to incorporate several generic strands into the narrative: in some sense the novels have aspects of the saga genre, but the historical reach into political and social contexts is immense and truly ambitious. Finally, central to the whole enterprise is an insistence on the intuitive insight of the regional writer into formative experience on the peripheral plane in a culture.

The motifs of land, sea, and sky are partly used in this structure, but at the core is the sense of the timeless. The standing stones overlooking the Blawearie land she inherits from her father come to symbolize this historical and mystical sweep of consciousness to which Chris returns at turning-points in her eventful life:

There were the standing stones, so seldom she'd seen them this last nine months. Cobwebbed and waiting they stood, she went and leant her cheek against the meikle one . . . it was strange and comforting—stranger still when you thought that this stone circle, more and more as the years went on at Kinraddie, was the only place where ever she could come and stand back a little from the clamour of the days.[31]

Clamor there certainly is in the novels, as Gibbon's writing comprehends the interplay of the emotional life and the desire for a sense of authentic being with the responsibility of a true community to guide its members to their fulfillment. Gibbon's Kinraddie begins with a long introduction to the cast of characters, and the keynote is large, Rabelaisian, energetic to the point of a grand scheme, hinting at national character and tradition alongside a partly grotesque vision of the uneasy community.

The first novel, *Sunset Song*, illustrates this encompassing energy, beginning with extended anecdotes with underlying humor, often surreal and threatening—as if there is an inner force of anarchy within Kinraddie, almost genetically placed, a latent unbalancing, unsettling element. The manual workers and farmers are contrasted with the crofters in the residual Highland communities further north (where Guthrie hails from). Added to this, there is the clash with "the English," the aristocracy, and the automobile—all threats in different ways to the unchanging moral and relational structures of the place.

Chris, as the protagonist, is repeatedly explained as being a composite of different identities, thus developing the now familiar sense of duality that Scottish writers feel. There is the English Chris and the Scottish Chris, but another version too, and that is the archetypal regional entity of the awakening spirit, sustained by the deeper levels of being suggested and sustained by the land and history. Gibbon integrates this sense of history in a robust, aggressive way in most places in order to maintain the sense of base conflict at the center of people as well as historical process. Chris's duality is explained most clearly with regard to education and "Englishness":

So that was Chris and her reading and schooling, two Chrisses there were that fought for her heart and tormented her. You hated the land and the coarse speak of the folk and learning was brave and fine one day; and the next you'd waken with the peewits crying across the hills, deep and deep, crying in the heart of you.[32]

Gibbon makes the Highland identity the most expressive instrument of this deeper level of being Scottish. In the prolonged account of Chris's wedding to Ewan, the Red Highlander gives a speech that rises beyond the limits of the social context and attains a poetic nature, as if he represents something essential and indefinably Scottish, behind the emotions as they all sing their folk songs and make their speeches in the barn at Blawearie: "he spoke fine, though funny with that Highland twist," and when he mentions the lovers, he says: "And when they passed to that other winter together they would know that was not the end of it, it was but a sleep that in another life would burgeon fresh from another earth."[33]

Gibbon's work, therefore, shows that version of the Scottish sense of duality which stresses the expansive, the panoramic: the sweep of society as a supportive, organic enterprise dealing with the larger world, whether that be the Great War, the "posh" outsiders, or simply the weight of political change. On the other hand, in Neil Gunn's *The Key of the Chest*, we have another textualization of a different communal commentary. Gunn's Caithness, distant and different in many important ways from the entrenched English creation of the Burns Night Scot or the Highland crofter, is given here as an enclosed, night-shrouded place that is regulated to the point of oppression. The plot-device of having a sailor's body washed up on shore with a chest of papers and an issue of possible murder creates a succession of inquiries into the nature of such a tough, self-sufficient community. The old man, Smeorach, seems to express this at the end of chapter 9:

Smeorach lifted his eyes to the blind window, and it seemed to him that life was all shadows, and the movement of shadows, and blindness, and had no meaning, and when you hearkened for its sound, it had no sound.[34]

In the ambiance of the novel, Gunn constantly includes fear, anticipation, the unknown stranger, the echoes from a larger-scale world, even though he points out the tendency of Scots to leave home and join the cosmopolitan movements.

In the end, the world of Sgeir and Kinraddie, the far north and the north of the English imagination or of the cultured, urban Scottish imagination is a composite of that duality that Scottish writers present in infinite varieties: night-enshrouded worlds yet below open skies, tightly netted communities yet looking outward for some other freedom. It is possible to see, in the Scottish regional genres, versions of regional belonging (fused with a nationalist narrative, of course, also) comparative to the English ones, but they have to deal with myths of separateness that are more extreme: the Gael, the Highlander, the Ploughman Poet, and the broad-backed farmer, dour and Calvinist—all residual myths in an imagined place, persisting in the popular sagas and films long after the simplistic Kailyard treatments of the subject have gone.

7

Imagining Wales: James Hanley, *The Welsh Sonata,* and the Anglo–Welsh Debate

With other varieties of regional writing now surveyed across the range of cultural contexts and with writers actually native to the area mostly in mind, we arrive at the issue of the imagined regional identity as constructed by an outsider—the invention grafted on, as it were, by an adopted native, an outside eye looking for kinship. Wales provides an ideal case study of this, as the history of writing about Wales in English has caused the recent bifurcation of terminology to express this category: first the phrase was Anglo–Welsh writing, and now, more generally, it is "Welsh literature in English." It is not difficult to find twentieth-century examples of these adopted children, the second-stance regional writers who impose patterns of meaning on a culture they understand from outside.

I have in front of me a signed copy of *The Welsh Sonata*, published in 1954. The book had been presented to one of Hanley's friends, and he had written this quotation from Pope's *Essay on Criticism*: "Words are like leaves and where they most abound, / much fruit of sense beneath is rarely found." In his impish way, he had added: "To Nina with love, after a happy meeting in the land of the Celts." This was Easter 1957; at this time, Hanley had lived in Wales for over twenty years.

The inscription has two notable points of interest for readers of Hanley. First, the quotation: it might be an epigraph as a prologue to his writing craft. His attitude to writing was clearly that of the craftsman with an innate sense of measurement and selection: just as a carpenter will instinctively choose the right wood and the proper dimensions for a task, so Hanley always seemed to select the suitable style and structure for his fictions. In his short stories, this ability to use only the apposite words and sentences for the immediate narrative focus is apparent: he seems to follow a voice and personality through to resolution.

The second point here is the phrase "land of the Celts": used in *The Welsh Sonata,* it gives a genuine hint about his attitude to his adopted home and its people. It reinforces the images we have of his life in Wales, not only from John Cowper Powys's letters, but also from Elizabeth Berridge's memoir, "Notes from the Boilerhouse."[1] In this, she gives an account of her husband's editing chores, done at the house in Llansantffraid that Hanley had found for them. The accompanying photographs show Hanley and his wife, Timmy, in their Llanfechain cottage and then with Powys at the 1936 Corwen Eisteddfod. "The land of the Celts" was, for Hanley, a place where he could have the creative spaces, internal and topographical, that he needed.

Working with Reginald Moore (the editor of *Modern Reading*), Hanley had found someone else to share the idyll. Berridge witnessed Hanley as a strong, extrovert character, relishing the locality. She talks about his dragging branches of trees and smashing them against the cottage wall, and she stresses his "love of simple games." He and Powys were made Bards to the Gorsedd.

In many respects, these images are typical of the foreigner in love with an adopted culture and, in literature, of the category of writer who becomes an artist of a special kind of imaginative borderland. Other examples are endless, but mention of Christopher Isherwood in California, Brian Moore in Canada, and Henry James in England provide parallels: writers who are drawn to impulses of creativity within the culture in which they settle. Of course, in Hanley's case, his life before Wales had entailed Ireland and then Liverpool, followed by war experience and sea travel. He had gathered an inordinate amount of "material" for fiction—life-data ready to be unloaded.

Hanley appears to have been insistent on certain elemental qualities of Welshness, something as profound as Lawrence's claims for his archetypal, blood-driven miners. In one of his very last works, *Against the Stream* (1982), he even has the enigmatic Welshman, Thomas, appear to promise, in the opening chapter, some central preoccupation with this soulful presence, but it is never developed. We find the same mystique in John Cowper Powys, perhaps expressed mostly plainly in

his diary entry for 23 May 1935, after making love: "Is it the amorousness of Wales—is it the aura of Owen Glendower's domain? Is it some
mysterious life-sap emanating from these hills and valleys?"

The question has to be asked: what version of Wales did he construct?
We could then ask why he did do so, and what sources or cognate
writings will help readers to understand a novel like *The Welsh Sonata*.

For we do need help. The novel is many things in one: a sustained
poetic narrative with Biblical diction and syntax, an allegory for the
human condition, an elegy for lost values, a projection of Hanley's own
isolation (a trademark in all his fiction), and, finally, an Anglo–Welsh
novel. I want to argue here that as the last of these possibilities, the
novel is placed within a certain tradition in Anglo–Welsh writing and
that a reading of the book enlightens many of the issues around the
notion of "Anglo–Welsh."

However, before developing this, it is worth returning to Elizabeth
Berridge and her assessment of Hanley. In her few critical comments,
she takes Powys's words as a guide;

Powys believed that every work of art is a purgation of the artist from
something poisonous in himself: "the really great things in writers of
genius," he wrote, "that will influence posterity are not those which are
premeditated and intended, but those which rise up from the depth of the
writer's unique soul and are suffused through his work." This quality he
found in James Hanley.[2]

A writer like Hanley would find the nature of the *Eisteddfod* and
its traditions of strictly formal, metrical compositions in the competitions for Bard very close to his own definition of writing. The poet, as
textualized in the Welsh literature, is represented as combining this
nature of disciplined literary skill with the view of art as something that
rises up "from the depth of the writer's unique soul."

The social and traditional image of the writer in Wales has always had
these fusions in mind. The poet in Dylan Thomas's *Under Milk Wood*,
Eli Jenkins, also has these qualities. He exemplifies this very personage,
even though Thomas is satirizing him in one way of reading the play. He
is writing alone, working on his intricate metrical poems, when the other
denizens of the imagined community are rising and active.[3] He illustrates that aspect of representation in Welsh writing that exists in contradistinction to realistic modes. In other words, how does a writer dealing
with a culture seen objectively, either from within or from a stranger's

viewpoint, achieve the authenticity required? This also challenges the conventional idea of what is realistic. Obviously, such features as senti-mentality and melodrama will always be potential parallel ingredients of a basically realistic mode, as when Dickens lifts his physical description of Coketown at the opening of *Hard Times* into a grotesque hyperbolic pattern of metaphor.

To add a dimension of self-referential narrative, Hanley's Goronwy Jones is the bard in the sense of the lesser figure: he is the writer who wants to enter the Eisteddfod contest, to take part in the more routine business of the poetic expression within institutions and social func-tions—not the pure poet of nature whom we have in Rhys.

Hanley, then, writing about Wales, clearly felt the need to adapt his own method of intense internalized feeling as a force to generate narra-tive interest in the Welsh setting. But he writes about Wales in English, and from the stance of a visitor. Even a long residence in Wales does not change the fact that the category of "Anglo–Welsh" would have to be applied. The term has been the subject of a long debate, sometimes quite heated, just as the cognate terms Anglo–Irish and Anglo–Scottish have. As a literary connotation it was first used by Idris Bell in 1922, but since then, with the fluctuations of intensity in the presence of Plaid Cymru in Welsh life and the bilingual development of the literature, "Anglo–Welsh" has come to inhabit a definite place, with a canon and a critical corpus of considerable standing.

The crux of the debate is well expressed by Raymond Garlick, in his defense of the duality of Welsh/Anglo–Welsh literatures: "The problem language in Wales is English. How did it get here? What is its role here? Can it be justified here? How should it be taught here? What should its status be here in relation to Welsh? . . . These are questions for the guardians and professionals of the language—the Anglo–Welsh writers, and after them, the teachers."[4] Garlick goes on to stress that judgments on Anglo–Welsh writing have been sociological rather than literary ones—that is, as Hanley's work shows, non-Welsh writers, along with Welsh-born writers who do not write in Welsh, produce commentaries, insights, and representations primarily with the need to place the land and the community at the center. To do this in English is the center of the problem. It raises issues of linguistic determinism: that identity and consciousness are only genuinely expressed through the language that is native to the experience: language and cognition going together in an intimate bonding.

We need to return here to Hanley's novel and his reasons for writing it. To distinguish between the cathartic or other personal impulses to write and the specifically Welsh-based ones is essential at this point. He had previously written about Wales from a documentary, sociological viewpoint in *Grey Children,* but that was a context of industry and universal human pain; now, in the later novel, he had faced the myth of Wales, imprinted on its actuality.

In an interview with his son, Liam, Hanley has this to say about the basis and beginnings of *The Welsh Sonata*:

The two interesting things I can say about the book is that it was my first ever excursion into the Welsh soul. I found Wales to be a beautiful country and it was really where my root went and still is there of course. I christened Wales "a country of kingdoms." It's the first time in my life as a writer that I'd abandoned writing with a pen because my work was all holograph.[5]

Hanley then relates the writing of *The Anatomy of Llangyllwch* and says, "I put together three Welsh syllables. . . . Llangyllwch is a purely contrived word."

These comments are helpful, yet also complex. Hanley was infatuated with the land, and then willed a native identity on himself. In the same transcript interview, he talks about baptizing himself in a stream: "There came a moment in my life as a writer living in Wales—in fact I was so happy one day walking up that mountain, that I stopped by a brook and I knelt down and baptized myself Welsh (laughs)."[6] The notion of seeing the "Welsh soul" and then actually wanting to "become" Welsh takes us far away from the idea of most writing characterized as "Anglo–Welsh" perhaps, but it does highlight some of Hanley's motivations in writing the novel. But the heart of the issue here are the specific representations in the novel and how they relate to two other similar works—J. M. Synge's *Playboy of the Western World* and Dylan Thomas's *Under Milk Wood.* Arguably, it is through comparison that we may find a way to explain the singularity of Hanley's vision in this novel. There is also a certain precedent for elements of Hanley's Biblical prose rhythms in Caradoc Evans's controversial collection of stories, *My People* (1915).

Again, in the conversation with Liam, Hanley gives the source of Rhys the Wound: "Actually Rhys the Wound was a real man who was a friend of mine . . . and I'll only make one comment about him . . . and that is that he would travel by bus or train . . . nobody would collect his fares. If he went into a pub, nobody would collect the money. . . . I christened him The Children's King."[7] Twice in the interview, Hanley talks of the writing of the novel as a "dream session," and here we have some guidance as a basis for criticism. If we assemble the commentary we have so far, then these are the facts: first, *The Welsh Sonata* emerged from an intense motivation to explain a quintessence of something of the "Welsh soul" as Hanley saw it; second, that he thought of himself as in some way integrated into the community; and, lastly, that Hanley was going through a process of creating his own version of "the land of the Celt." Therefore, the autobiographical basis of the novel lies in the creative sustenance behind a powerful fusion of an imagined Wales, a universal, oral-rooted narrative, and the actual person of Rhys the Wound, the "Children's King" who had represented some notable human qualities to Hanley's imagination.

The novel is an impassioned yet stylized, rhetorical account of a community. In choosing biblical rhythms in his syntax, Hanley had, probably unwittingly, adopted a method used by Caradoc Evans in *My People,* a collection of stories published in 1915 and based on an actual community, Rhydlewis in Cardiganshire, a nonconformist locality. Evans, a draper turned journalist who left rural Wales for London, wrote about his home community in such a way that there was an uproar. To many he had betrayed Wales rather than given it to the world. To others, he had produced something totally reprehensible, as described in chapter five.

John Harris, in his scholarly edition of the book, summarizes the response in Wales like this:

For the majority of his compatriots, the author of *My People* had alienated himself utterly (as he predicted, their hatred had pursued him beyond the grave). Caradoc, too, stuck to his position. Less than three years before his death, he wrote of a "certain religious clique in Wales" for whom "the supernatural is everything and human charity nothing."[8]

Evans had depicted the community as unfeeling, hard, and riddled with prejudice and narrowminded attitudes. But the point here is that it was expressed as a powerful and spare prose realism, so intense that it bordered on allegory, and often so visual and explicit in its depiction of suffering that it shocked like a Biblical story—part of his intention.

Like Hanley, Evans had a vision of an imagined Wales, superimposed on the actual topography and social community. Again like Hanley, his language is minimal, and he is liberal with implication and poetic effect. One story, "Be This Her Memorial," may exemplify the nature of this rhetoric. It is the story of the death of Nanni. Evans presents the reader with an outline in the opening paragraph, and this sets the tone and sentence structure for the story:

Mice and rats, as it is said, frequent neither churches nor poor men's homes. The story I have to tell you about Nanni—the Nanni who was hustled on her way to prayer meeting by the Bad Man, who saw the phantom mourners bearing away Twm Tybach's coffin, who saw the spirit hounds and heard their moanings two days before Isaac Penparc took wing—the story I have to tell you contradicts that theory.[9]

It is interesting to compare this with:

Now a man is free to do as he wills, and if he is in a free country, then I suppose he is free to let his hair grow on his head until it's just a lovely cloud. But there's a reason for it, I have no doubt, and many a time I've seen the cloud moving about this place.[10]

This is from *The Welsh Sonata*, early in the text. Both passages adopt the intonation of the Welsh vernacular rhythms; both access anecdotal narrative; both adopt an overarching metaphorical trope in which to give the significance of the story, as in oral literature and as in the Bible. Hanley, like Evans, is following a deep compulsion to impose a spiritual narrative onto a quasi-realistic physical setting—in Hanley's case, following "a dream."

Here, then, is the heart of the question: the issue of the authentic and the rhetorical in prose and dialogue. It is a matter of to what extent a writer stands on tiptoe for effects of vocabulary, intonation, and rhythm. Thomas Hardy had been plagued by this issue with regard to the realism in his dialogue involving his countrymen, and it tends to be a problem in any writing in which the vernacular is prominent. Arguably, one of the most representative works in this respect is Synge's drama, *The Playboy of the Western World*, produced at the Abbey Theatre in 1907, when a week of rioting followed the performance. This was linked with what was called "wild language" by Lady Gregory and also with the strange morality and heroism around supposed patricide. But much of the furor stemmed from the stylistic effects of the peasants' language.

Basically, Synge's vision entails linguistic expression embedded in a rich sinewy metaphor that fuses the earthiness of rural life in the west of Ireland with a grand poetry of potent sensuous expression. T. R. Henn summarizes it in this way: "The work of Synge is slight in bulk, but it is a unity.... The poems show his concern with Villon and the Eliza- bethans, and with that timbre that 'has its roots among clay and worms.' ... Life oscillates between the mystery of the poetic vision and the brutal realities of living."[11] This could be an explanation of the effects Hanley aims at. In Synge's play we have the ordinary peasants saying,

Christy: How would a lovely, handsome woman the like of you be lone- some when all men should be thronging around to hear the sweetness of your voice, and the little infant children should be pestering your steps, I'm thinking, and you walking the roads.[12]

Hanley similarly uses emphatic phrases, repeated parallel constructions, and nonstandard syntax to express not simply a sense of region but a cognitive, individuated rhythm to match the Welsh "difference":

He was as powerful as two lions with jaws locked hard upon the same bone and each pulling his way. And stronger than the steel of Huw Ellis's great wheel held fast and bound on the tenth of March, and any movement sealed by ice and fire of the air on that hardest day.[13]

The usual underpinning of such writing is a gap between characters thinking in their first language and expressing themselves in their sec- ond language. Hence, Synge's peasants' words and sentences may be explained by the Gaelic syntax beneath; the same could be said for Hanley's, but of course he was not a Welsh speaker. The effects are therefore an uneasy mix of secondhand speech rhythms and the literary residues of previous reading in Hanley's creative mind.

Therefore, Hanley's incantation of similes extended from the above quotation follows the expression of certain Biblical (Authorized Ver- sion) tropes and superimposes the result of the well-explored skill of the writer's acute ear for dialogue.

Dylan Thomas not only uses his own version of this, often in the words given to Captain Cat, but he also sends it up, with Eli Jenkins's consummate parody of the pastoral–regional elegy, which he writes in a simplistic tetrameter, a parody of amateur versifying,[14] alongside Captain Cat's description of the women in the spring morning.[15]

Thomas is giving us a simile close to authentic vernacular here, and in Jenkins's poem we have the purely literary. Of course, in the Welsh language there are cognate forms of vernacular and literary. Hanley the bard would be well aware of this, and one answer to the puzzles of the rhythms and syntax in *The Welsh Sonata* is that Hanley is attempting to show us the "soul" of Wales as being defined by its need for an aesthetic dimension to being, a desire for existential voices defining its being in the world.

Hence Rhys the Wound becomes an allegorical and a quasi-realistic figure at once: "He was a country child, Mister Jones, and they say he first saw the light of day through a rabbit's ear."[16] This can be convincing as authentic vernacular, or it may be stylized and concocted, but the literary issue is one of the grand design, not the verisimilitude. This reinforces the well-entrenched notion in art of what Goethe called *Dichtung und Wahrheit*—truth and "design." Literary language takes us into the realm of "design," the artificial. Truth, in Goethe's sense, is the actual life-data of the experience. If we accept that a writer can never reproduce this "truth," then all writing is an attempt to place a secondary vision in order to locate the artist's own sense of the "truth." Synge and Hanley did this through prose rhythms and a mixing of vernacular and rhetorical; what makes Hanley's novel so remarkable is that he sustained that stylistic tour de force for a novel; more suitable genres are short plays, meditative poems, or short stories.

All this matches well with the concept of a sonata. Most dictionaries note that a sonata is basically two voices in interplay, often through three movements. Hanley the musician, the pianist, enjoyed playing with this in the specific literary context of having fun with narrative devices. Therefore, the basis of the novel is the dual presence of Goronwy Jones, policeman and authorial voice. This enables Hanley to do what he does best: earthy but spare dialogue, as in the visit to the "Saturday town" pub to talk to Flook and the woman with the head wound. This element in the novel brings Hanley close to Dylan Thomas's technique of impressionistic nightscape, perhaps stemming from *The Waste Land*, and Hanley shows his mastery of this technique:

And they moved for the darkness chained to the ground. Out into the burling and bloody Saturday airs.

The closing time shouts shot out from many a doorway and split the air about them, and they walked quickly, and the wind behind them.

They talked.

"Is there no bus your way home sir?"

"No bus."

Their voices rose on two quite different levels of air.[17]

In this way Jones is deftly placed in the wider community in Hanley's subtext of making a dialectic between the Wales of myth, poetry and the aesthetic impulse and the Wales of the towns and the "English." References to both are always negative and condemnatory: "Think of them towns, the walls, everywhere,"[18] or "May have got him drunk in a foreign pub over the Border . . . and then laughed under the table by the English."[19]

With these various techniques as a foundation, the poetic narrative itself then challenges the reader to frame an interpretation of Wales. Hanley's aim to write about the "Welsh soul," although clearly a personal creative quest, has a basis in this dialogic interplay between the author's presence and the figure of Jones. The ploy enables Hanley to move deftly from realistic settings to his allegorical style. The motifs repeated are largely biblical and often follow such notable features as the deictic structures of colloquial speech, as in "that Meirion and his mad son" or "And that Bagillt man opened wide his eyes."[20]

Such simple representation through nonstandard language forms an irresistible mix with the rhetoric, and the "sonata" is also perhaps, in another sense, this linguistic interplay as well as the bipolar workings of author and character. Following the notion of "sonata" itself, it becomes quite complex. Perhaps only a learned musicologist could pursue this, but in terms of style, much of what Synge had to create through artifice is here in abundance, too. The parallel sources of Aran Islands and Galway for Synge and of Wales for Hanley make a profitable inquiry for criticism.

Changing the perspective on *The Welsh Sonata* and looking at the book within the context of Hanley's work generally, it is one markedly concerned with a response to late Modernism. In its methods of narrative it challenges the limitations of the ordered page and the strict format. It even tries to stretch the power of implication and partial interior knowledge given, say, in Woolf or in Joyce's *Dubliners.* There is a hint of this approach in a statement made by Sir Flook: "I could tell you a summer's tale . . . and of a man–child with his hands cupped in the early morning to catch the sunlight. That tale should be close to a fire and the wind howling."[21] The *Winter's Tale* is, as Shakespeare's Mamilius says, for winter and is sad. Hanley's tale is an allegory of a redemptive life. Rhys the Wound is somewhere between Christ and "some mute, inglorious Milton" or representative scapegoat figure. He is King of the Children, an idiot savant, a Lord of Misrule, and it is clear that Hanley wants to stress the isolation, bard-like, within but not of the community, as Dylan Thomas depicts his poet as a man who work at producing intricate metrical verse in his lonely chapel, aspiring to succeed at the National Eisteddfod.[22]

The stereotypes are there, but Hanley takes on the fragmentation and interiority of Modernism, to meld it to a sustained poem, restless with the conventional sentence and the dominant Standard English word order. There is a ubiquity of metaphor in every breath almost, so that figurative lexis acts to erase or minimize the functional and structural words.

Finally, and typically in the case of Hanley, the last sections of the novel then proceed to undermine the grand statements of the main search for Rhys and the meetings with Sir Flook. In the chapter giving a "verbatim report on a steam of abuse from that Mrs. B. Prothero, late of Llangar" (p. 173) we have what could be defined as a Postmodern appropriation of the ironic manner written almost as a parody of itself. This interpolation has the effect of a raw bathos, almost disarming the reader after the rhetorical tropes and patterns of imagery in the central narrative. We suddenly feel the presence of Jones the ordinary artist looking for a suitably "high" subject for his *Eisteddfod* poem. The passage has the same effect as the porter at the gate in *Macbeth*:

The lava was choking my sitting room and it was like a fog in the place, and I had just enough of it by this time I can tell you. I got to my feet and I shouted to her that I had had enough of it.[23]

Reading this section juxtaposed with the scene in which Rhys finds Olwen and Parry making love exemplifies the paradox of the novel: the aim is clearly to achieve the effects we find in Caradoc Evans and Synge, with a bold attempt to make a statement about Wales and some of her ideologies; yet finally, the novel also rushes from the Modernist effect of the scene in the hut to the bathos of the simple realism of the bar and the dining room. What Alan Ross said about Hanley's sailors is helpful here: "These characters are like the figures sculptured by Henry Moore—still, enduring people, under sentence of history, confined by the rhythms of sleep and exhaustion, but dreaming action under the bone."[24]

The Welsh Sonata offers a definitive version of Hanley's central fictional concern: the examination of a community and its failure to absorb the individuated inner lives of the creatures locked in themselves. Just as the metaphors of the oceans were always available to him, as to Conrad, as instruments of his craft, so the "soul" of Wales as he saw it and felt it appealed as an organizing principle. But the community here is poeticized in a deliberate, often uneasy prose sitting alongside a tactile realism. In this he is comparable to a particular strand of Anglo–Welsh writing that insists on mythologizing the Welsh rural communities, from Evans to the figure of Cynddlyan in R. S. Thomas's poetry.

To end with the relation of such writing to the debate on what constitutes the varieties of Anglo–Welsh writing, it cannot be avoided that Hanley was cut off linguistically from his subject here, so we have an artist's vision. Arguably, *Under Milk Wood* and *My People* are just as much visions and myths as interpretations of observed data. The data are there; just as Rhys was a real tramp, so Thomas's Eli Jenkins was most probably based on the Rev. Orchwy Bowen of New Quay."[25] But, essentially, Hanley's Wales is very much another arena constituted of an indifferent universe and a huddled mass of humanity calling itself a community. Through the loners and rejects, the broken men and the wanderers, his devices are catalysts for the fissures within the apartment houses and institutions of the physical world the individual has to access. As in Hanley's story, "People are Curious," in which the trek to find a brother and a job ends in uncomfortable revelations about the human potential for hardness and cruelty, so this ambitious novel reaches for two narratives at once: first, a story of a lone magical nomad and, second, an inner truth about a spiritual place, a Wales somehow sacred and yet fallen. Ironically, where the inner meanings of Rhys should be what the bard explains and retells, the result is more a conventional document of a mere observer, a Boswell skilled in meticulous recording of the inexplicable.

Jones is perhaps Hanley as compulsive writer, and Rhys may be the mythical artist within; but Jones is enriched by his ordinariness, and his often overreaching vocabulary eventually demonstrates that the English language may be sufficient to the task when Wales is to be somehow revealed, either in reality or in myth. But this will always have to be asserted with an awareness that Hanley unwittingly wrote a novel that can be aligned with the Wales represented in Evans and Thomas. As M. Wynn Thomas says:

With *My People*, *Kulturkampf* began in Wales with a vengeance, and for a generation thereafter Anglo–Welsh writing seemed to Welsh language writers to bear the mark of Caradoc like the Mark of the Beast.[26]

8

The New Northerners: Studies of Provincial Life

In Richard Hoggart's influential study of working-class culture, *The Uses of Literacy* (1957), he depicts the homely relational structures of his own people in Hunslet, Leeds, in the middle of the twentieth century. He stresses that "The more we look at working-class life, the more we try to reach the core of the working-class attitudes. The more surely does it appear that the core is the sense of the personal, the concrete, the local."[1] His profile of the community may be seen as a basement view of that rich edifice of Northern culture asserted and examined in the subgenre of "Northern writing" appearing in the late 1950s.

The main works usually cited are certainly not all set in Yorkshire. Alan Sillitoe's *Saturday Night and Sunday Morning* (1958) is based in Sillitoe's Nottingham, and Bill Naughton's plays and stories are set in Lancashire. But the core of novels and stories that John Braine, Stan Barstow, David Storey, and Barry Hines produced in the years between 1958 and 1968 have established a hermetic, closely circumscribed body of work with a range of attitudes and subjects in common.

Of course, the "angry young men" dramatists were also peripheral to the fiction, in the sense of regional consciousness, and perhaps the most relevant work here is Arnold Wesker's *Roots* (1959)—"relevant" in the sense that all the Northern novelists had to cope with the issue of how to reconcile the variety of imagery and narrative traditions of "Northern" writing with the massive changes in popular culture and education happening in their time. Hoggart's Hunslet is described as a community sustained by close communication and hierarchies; mother and father are as much ideological concepts as authority figures, and there is an oral tradition located here as strong as anything in folklore or in the novels of D. H. Lawrence and Hardy.

The new Northerners had to reconcile the appeal of this entrenched regional culture with that of America, with the new attraction of social mobility, and with moral and sexual revolutions also. Whereas in Hoggart the recreation is small-scale, being the club and pub at the most, for the new protagonists of Barstow or Braine we have the gradual encroachment of middle-class or even bohemian culture. In *A Kind of Loving* (1960) Vic Brown's workmate talks about seeing an "arty" French film, Joe Lampton joins the thespians, and Billy Casper reads a book on falconry while at a secondary modern school in South Yorkshire.

These "Northerners" are also given a label that illustrates the continuing difficulty of definition and English mind-set with regard to any writing north of the Home Counties. As early as 1898, Arnold Bennett opened his novel *A Man from the North* with a reference to "the North Country," and he meant Staffordshire. Sillitoe's Nottingham is hardly "Northern" in the sense implied by the traditional use of north applied to the Humber–Trent–Severn division. Therefore, in an interesting twist of semantic application, "the new Northern novel" that critics spoke about in the 1950s shows the persistence of this concept: "Northern" in fact became a synonym for "provincial" in common usage. The poets and playwrights emerging from Liverpool, or Sid Chaplin in Northumberland, for instance, could just as easily be categorized within this central group.

A feature of the Yorkshire writing at the core of this work is often overlooked: how it compared to the attitudes and representations of the older generation of Yorkshire writers still active at the beginning of the decade. For instance, Phyllis Bentley's novel, *Crescendo*, appeared in 1958, and it concerns—as much of her fiction did—a cluster of families and their experience across the decades from late-Victorian Britain to the post-1945 period. The basis of Bentley's work, as those of Priestley, Holtby, and Lettice Cooper, had always been to be panoramic and comprehensive and to interweave explanatory social history and *Weltanschauung*. This all emanated from a sense of middle-class values and a cultural focus to match that of London. Much of the ethos behind

Crescendo, for example, is the rise of talent through hard work and proper right thinking. Bentley is interested in political fair-mindedness, thrift, learning, and cooperation. The Yorkshire she has in mind is something tractable in the hands of the novelist: something malleable in terms of a conventional theme stemming from Victorian constructions of the fabric of regional life.

Bentley's basis is explained in her autobiography, *O Dreams, O Destinations* (1962), in which she celebrates the Yorkshire in her mind, the source of her storytelling. After discussing the rival claims of London and Yorkshire as bases for creative work, she writes:

> At once, it seemed, my decision justified itself. I had arranged to go home for a few days in connection with the shooting of the film *We of the West Riding*. For which I had provided the scenario. . . . The film moved me strongly, especially the singing of the Hallelujah Chorus from Handel's *Messiah* in a small moorland chapel.[2]

Bentley notes that this music, heard over a crowd scene of workers coming out of a Halifax mill, reminded her of the quintessential Yorkshire. In her diary at the time, when she writes with joy about Yorkshire, it is in the context of the Halifax Thespians, *Yorkshire Post* articles, and her space to work in. In other words, her Yorkshire is marooned in an invented Yorkshire, a heightened, attractive place without the current (1950s) urgency of the clash of generations and the challenge of a new race called "teenagers" and a class of young working-class people who were beginning to go to university and absorb new ideas.

Bentley was aware of this, and in her autobiography she describes the new Yorkshire folk as "thoroughly dissatisfied" and with "a code of ethics as yet unformulated."[3] She was coming to terms with the arrival of the new realism, given generally in the first person, packed with current slang (in *A Kind of Loving*, girls are called "bints"—an Arabic word absorbed by soldiers in Aden and Palestine). When Priestley explained Bentley's ability, it was in terms of expressing the "character" of West Riding people. In other words, that need to generalize on the indefinable traits developed in relation to environment persisted. He goes on to stress that she explored the social context "in depth, historically, economically, sociologically and psychologically, and turned herself into an original modern novelist."[4] Undoubtedly she did, but she has come to represent that variety of Yorkshire writing which wants to interpret "character" through history, politics, and the universally human in constant interplay, with the novelist as omniscient. The new Northerners built in the critique of that invention of tradition.

One of the most notable transitions in the reinvention of "the North" as the material for regional writing was the move from quasi-pastoral, elegiac modes to the attempt at a fresh, revisionist presentation of what would now be called sexual politics. Where the previous generation had still been interested in the centrality of romantic and idealistic affections in the social fabric, the new writers voiced the difficulties involved in renegotiating the rituals of courtship and sexual relations. In contrast, it is noticeable that the presence of nature and environment recedes in the decade of the "angry young men."

In most of these 1950s narratives, there is a bipolar set of oppositions, all centered on the generations confronting each other and on modernity. In the short stories of Barstow and Sillitoe, the older characters are either mentally scarred by the experience of the 1930s and the Second World War or unable to escape what Joyce would call the "paralysis" of their ideological frameworks and cultural habits. At the wedding in the opening chapter of *A Kind of Loving*, Vic has to advise his father not to wear brown shoes with a blue suit. In *Room at the Top*, Joe's landlady, Mrs. Thompson, is firmly defined in the narrow mind-set of the mother-figure, who bakes and is familiar with the shops and bus-routes. More strikingly, Sillitoe's Robboe—a workmate of Arthur Seton on the milling machines—is trapped in the small preoccupations of caring for equipment and working out wages. John Braine's Joe Lampton is constantly critical of the small regional boundaries of identity. He, perhaps more than the other protagonists in these works, is able to articulate the criticisms at the heart of that generation's restlessness: "I came to Warley on a wet September morning with the sky the grey of Guiseley sandstone. I was alone in the compartment. I remember saying to myself: 'No more zombies, Joe, no more zombies.'"[5]

In Arnold Wesker's *Roots* we have arguably the most explicit and profound exploration of that inextricable mix of regional identity and the culture of the working class. Hoggart's words on Hunslet, in which he notes that the argot of everyday communication is a strength and a preserver of communal feeling, is in Wesker dangerously double-edged. In the play, Beatie expatiates on the liberating nature of language—but it is a language beyond the comprehension of her Norfolk family, entrenched in poverty and ignorance. Her final tirade on their apathy expresses far more confidently and powerfully much of the critical stance taken up by the "angry young men" of Braine and Barstow:

Oh yes, we turn on a radio or a TV set maybe, or we go to the pictures—if them's love stories or gangsters—but isn't that the easiest way out? Anything so long as we don't have to make an effort. Well am I right? You know I'm right. Education ent only books and music—it's asking questions, all the time. There are millions of us, all over the country, and no one, not one of us, is asking questions.[6]

Repeatedly, in the "new Northern" writing of this time, the issue at the center is dissent. Randall Stevenson has suggested that, along with Kenneth Allsop's assessment, the writers here should be seen as "dissentient" rather than "angry" young men.[7] But the dissent in the context of the regional belonging so strongly established in Bentley and others creates an interesting ambivalence, and one of the clearest statements of this is in John Braine's *Room at the Top*. The specific importance of this novel is that the town of Warley, where Joe Lampton arrives to "remake" himself, is constantly compared to his home in another northern town, Dufton—ironically playing on the slang word "duff," perhaps. Where Warley has a certain cultural aspiration, Dufton has been representative of the worst stereotypes readers have of a Yorkshire industrial place, wrecked by economic forces. Braine gives a neat comparison of the two places: "Warley had never suffered very deeply from the slump; its eggs were in too many baskets. Three quarters of the working population of Dufton were unemployed in 1930. I remember the streets full of men with faces pasty from bread and margarine . . . and that river thick and yellow as pus."[8]

Braine is attempting to write about a new version of aspiration, explaining at once why the thespians of Warley look to the London stage as the epitome of sophistication, yet also examining the crippling inheritance of industrial unrest and urban decline. Most of the novelists offer as their dominant version of what is to replace the past limitations and passivity an uneasy fusion of sexual and ideological liberation, but the cramping morality of provincial England is never far away. In fact, the community of which Hoggart wrote was the same as the one that forms the basis of, for instance, Walter Greenwood's *Love on the Dole* (1933): Greenwood's Salford and Hoggart's Hunslet depended on self-help and individual responsibility for survival. Any hint of dissent was condemned, as any disturbance may potentially ruin the basis of the human exchanges of trust and interdependence. This same traditional ideology is the one from which the courtships, weddings, abortions, deaths, and affairs of the "new Northern" writing arise. Vic Brown's Ingrid becomes pregnant, and Vic has been too shy to ask for contraceptives: the new young man has a long way to go.

But that same historical inheritance is also a strength—a provider of that sense of permanence and dependability. The only real issue here is in the way that the protagonists objectify it all and take up a macho stance. In the end, it is as if "the North" and its working-class culture inevitably stultifies; the closed minds do so for safety. Braine, for instance, when referrin to a character "moving south," includes the predictable and the routine as factors in defining the sense of belonging in modernity:

"Do you know, when I come into this pub, I don't even have to order? They *automatically* issue a pint of wallop. And if I come in with someone else I point at them and nod twice if it's bitter." . . . He looked at his pint with an expression of comic gluttony on his plump, strangely cherubic face. "Lovely. Lovely ale" he said, "The mainstay of the Industrial North."[9]

The 1950s novels of Braine, Sillitoe, Barstow, and Storey point to a society on the cusp of radical change from within. The traditional macho values of the working-class male, stoical, afraid of emotion and commitment, indicate an urgent need to transmute into some other more satisfying cultural niche for the energy and vitality of the new generation. It is a simple matter to point to macrocosmic factors such as the cold war, the massive impact of American culture, and the residual moral vacancy of the war generation, just out of rationing and tired after so huge a scale of deprivation and ordeal. Yet the spirit of the era was one of daring to dip a toe into the unfamiliar dark waters of escape: Beatie's warning to her parents, the intellectual from London who has seen the wider world and the metropolitan values, is the voice of the new Northern protagonist: keen to break the shackles but unable to step out of the mold of his ancestors.

Everything is so small through the eyes of these young Northerners. The environment on most of this fiction and drama is one of a spiritual as well as an environmental and cultural impoverishment. Braine, for instance, makes the natural world around Warley more prominent than

Barstow or Sillitoe in their respective works referred to earlier; at times this condition is almost symbolic, as when Lampton has been thinking negatively about Dufton again. Lampton reflects that Warley has shown him a new way of living, made him "involved in its life," and as he walks in Dufton, we have this: "There were cigarette ends and orange peel and sweet wrappers in the gutter but no-one living had smoked those cigarettes or eaten those sweets; the town reminded me of those detective stories . . . which used to be complete with clues."[10] The river beneath him ran faster as he reflected, and "the bridge was swaying and creaking beneath my feet, and I suddenly was afraid that it might deliberately throw me into the water."[11]

These major novels of the period define a particular feeling of dissent about perhaps the most persistent version of regional invention: the industrial north. This is so profoundly complex now that it has been parodied almost into melodrama and surreal genres. One problem here is that the popular film versions of the central novels—*Saturday Night and Sunday Morning*, *Room at the Top*, and *A Kind of Loving*, in particular—have become an aggregate of "Northern sensibility" and treated almost like forerunners of the recent working-class writing from the distant periphery of the wild estates and run-down communities shifting and reshaping at the mercy of market forces.

In fact, one novel in particular departed from the "new Northerners" of the 1950s and related Yorkshire life much more tangibly to working-class experience, with practically no lip-service paid to the invented Yorkshire, post-Brontë. This is Barry Hines's *A Kestrel for a Knave* (1968), where we encounter a certain element of the destruction of regional belonging: the human nexus in society disintegrates. Billy Casper's story is one of a reclamation of values, and the catalyst is nature. Hines makes the theme of bonding by instinct and empathy something compensatory, a force to counteract the dissolution of the human community. Billy is disaffected: his own family exploits him and reduces him to servant and victim, his school defines him as a failure. Then, unlike the protagonists of the previous works discussed here, he is reclaimed through natural beauty, through a vision of attachment stronger than anything offered by people.

Hines deftly depicts a borderland, a place left behind by modernity but at the same time a casualty of it. With genuine economy of language and style, Hines develops an authentic account of a vestigial framework of instinctive belonging, and his surface anti-pastoral region—post-industrial Yorkshire—is almost a place of fallen grace. The hawk, like Hopkins's "Windhover," arrests attention with its beauty. But Hines is also strong with his ironical setting, as we move from the estate to a rural vision to equal those of Romantic poetry:

The sun was up and the cloud band in the East had thinned to a line on the horizon, leaving the dome of the sky clear. The air was still and clean, and the trilling of larks carried far over the fields of hay. . . . Great rashes of buttercups spread across the fields.[12]

In some ways similar to Dickens's juxtapositions of the schoolroom and the circus in *Hard Times*, Hines makes the school experience reductive: the abrupt, minimal, but pointedly critical passages dealing with the learning situation match the real emotional and aesthetic growth we see in Billy's work with Kes.

When Billy ventures into the night to catch the bird in its nest in the monastery wall, we have an affirmation of that long tradition in regional writing which relates the search for authentic living and being with the power of nature rather than with man-made things. His instinct has led him to something he can control, but by genuine teaching—a process of sharing and caring—as opposed to the authoritarian behavior of the head at Billy's school, who, when caning pupils, is given despairing commentary by Hines on the long failure of English social cohesion:

I've taught in this city for over thirty-five years now; many of your parents were pupils under me in the old city schools before this estate was built; and in all those years I'm certain that I've never encountered a generation as difficult to handle as this one. I thought I understood young people.[13]

Where Beatie's lecture failed, and where the attempts at articulate authenticity of being failed the "Northern males" of the 1950s revolt, Billy Casper achieves the fluency and confidence of real language in explaining his moral growth and his validation of his imagination through an instrument of nature. When he talks about the bird to Mr. Farthing, we have this:

"Trained it? I thought you had to be an expert to train hawks."
   "Well I did it."
   "Was it difficult?"
   "Course it was. You've to be right . . . right patient wi' 'em and take your time."[14]

And when Billy explains his teaching, the expression is close to the verbal richness and potency of poetry:

"Well, what you do is, you train 'em through their stomachs. You can only do owt wi' 'em when they're hungry, so you do all your training at feeding time."[15]

What is most striking about Northern writing in the years between 1958 and 1968 is that it was coming to terms with an unacknowledged but powerful tendency to textualize anything regional as an ill-defined frontier between civilized values and the power-base. But as the developments in television also made use of the new talent from writers with university educations and working-class families, so the "Play for Today" and the new realism of documentary drama made the literature more aware of the urgency of the political element in perceiving and inventing a region on the page. That is, although in mass-market fiction such genres as family sagas and Catherine Cookson's "clogs and shawls" novels were finding plenty of readers, the revisiting of regional life as something that had either been neglected entirely or had been changed beyond all recognition went on at a great pace—so much so that when writers began to take a renewed interest in locality and the transmutation of a sense of belonging into something more unreliable and whimsical, the "regions" of Victorian Britain were no longer circumscribed.

In fact, the anti-regional in *A Kestrel for a Knave* or in *Room at the Top* is often concerned with insisting that the definable area has gone, and a featureless waste-land has stepped in. Once again, nature as an all-embracing force is included, but this time, unlike for Wordsworth, it is the twentieth-century version of the global uniformity advancing into traditional fastnesses of local identity, so every northern settlement has its video shop, its garage, its post office, and so on. In the final assessment, what this writing brought was a sense of interiority, of well-defended and decorated moral chambers of domesticity and traditional family values. As Paul Barker noted in a review of Stan Barstow's autobiography, *In My Own Time*:

Now in his seventies, Barstow recalls a West Riding where you detected the shades of working class status by checking the cleanliness of doorsteps and windows. . . . Barstow says that, after some false starts, he decided to write about what he knew best: "The life of a 'lace-curtain' working-class family."[16]

It is often forgotten that the period immediately after the Second World War left a generation with their hopes for a better world pinned firmly on their children. This meant sacrifices, safety, and a reliance on the only "certainties" that had helped them to survive. Primary among these was "roots"—attaining as much of a sense of permanence as possible. Hence so much of the anger and criticism of 1950s writing in the North of England was about resisting this and taking risks. What was seen as a constant in the war against stability was place: locality became a word as small as the morality that seemed to be peddled as part of the "deal" of being young in such a borderland between what was modern and what was "safe."

9

Beyond London:
Poetry in Britain from the Periphery, 1945–1970

In 1995, one of the few books devoted to nonmetropolitan poetry in Britain was published by the University of Wales. This was *Poetry in the British Isles*, edited by Hans-Werner Ludwig and Lothar Fietz. The range and variety of the contents hint at the awesome complexity confronting anyone trying to see patterns and trends in this body of writing. There are contributions on marginal figures, place in poetry, Welsh, Anglo–Welsh, Scottish, Irish, and regional English poetry. What emerges from this is simply how profoundly the feeling for place, region, and difference is evident in this diversity. The essays collected in the anthology reflect the survival of both national and regional consciousness, and also the problematic of deciding what happened to regional poetry in the second half of the twentieth century.

A long series of influential Penguin anthologies published during this period further confuses the situation. What were the various editors to do with the inevitable individualists like Norman Nicholson or R. S. Thomas, who insisted on staying at home for their material? After all, the impact of Eliot, Pound, and Auden, inter alia, has made the lyric and to some extent the narrative poem appear to be essentially intellectual, cerebral: poetry accessible by means of colloquial diction and simple syntax, direct in statement and concerned with matter more than with manner was causing critical problems in the years after 1950. The various editors at Penguin tried to organize the richness and diversity emanating from all parts of Britain, and it became clear by the late 1960s that Irish and Scottish writers had claimed a particularly solid presence on the literary scene, even in the London publishing houses.

A. Alvarez, in his *The New Poetry* (1962), for instance, includes some notable American writers and gives substantial space to the new arrivals—R. S. Thomas, Larkin, Gunn, Hughes, and Redgrove. Alvarez's brief literary history offered in the introduction makes it clear that the scene has been "savage with gang warfare," and he wants to restore poetry "to the realm of common sense." Much of his discussion is about technique. When he deals with subject matter, it is either in terms of intellectual preoccupations, such as the impact of Freud, or on the nature of London and the establishment. But Alvarez feels it necessary to offer a certain polemic: "What poetry needs . . . is a new seriousness. I would define this seriousness simply as the poet's ability and willingness to face the full range of his experience with his full intelligence . . . since Freud, the dichotomy between emotion and intelligence has become totally meaningless."[1] Now, in the contents of his anthology, Alvarez was rightly giving the reader a balance of the established and the innovative. But the preoccupation with "intelligence" and the quality of density of language to convey accurate observation and insight into universalities is assumed. In other words, as he was reflecting thus on the poets from universities and clubs, there was another aesthetic emerging, and it was largely from the cultural periphery. Larkin's early work had just appeared, and he was partly interested in delineating Humberside, and "the North" generally, as a place indicative of both a modern malaise and a limbo—almost a sense of "*et in Arcadia ego*" but with that sweet melancholy that proves so productive in exile.

But exile from the cultural center or from "where it happens" need not be linked to either the avant-garde or indeed to the younger poets nurtured by the establishment in the poetry world. A massive revolution happened—a radical repositioning and a fresh comprehensive concept of British poetry twenty years later, in Blake Morrison and Andrew Motion's anthology, *The Penguin Book of Contemporary British Poetry*. By that point, several things have become clear: first, that the notion of a "canon" is becoming untenable; second, that something we call Postmodern has impacted on "standards" in art; and finally, that several new voices from the more distant parts of Britain had arrived by 1970. These latter writers include Douglas Dunn, Tony Harrison,

Seamus Heaney, Tom Paulin, Paul Muldoon, Craig Raine, and Fleur Adcock. Of a total of twenty poets in the volume, six are Irish.

One of the most recent anthologies, Sean O'Brien's *The Firebox: Poetry in Britain and Ireland after 1945* (1998), goes even further and begins the process of trying to assimilate the deep and challenging impact of Irish and Scottish poets on the scene generally in the previous fifty years. This time, thirty-five poets here are Irish or Scottish, and most of them take social, cultural, and historical themes from their nations as explicit elements in their work. A few English regional writers, such Ian McMillan and Simon Armitage in Yorkshire, are included by 1998. But on the whole, most ambitious large-scale anthologies dealing with these years take note of the marked presence of non-English writers. My list above, by the way, includes no mention of the poetry coming from ethnic minorities and so on.

This preamble is to stress how important the central, parallel currents of writing were in British poetry up to 1970. The thirty years dealt with here saw the school of Auden decline, then the rise of the Movement, followed by notably original poets who arrived with certain collections that have proved, with hindsight, to have heralded many of the trends and influences reflected in O'Brien's and Motion's anthologies. The sheer multiplicity of voices was not there with such a breadth of peripheral diversity in the years from 1950 to 1970. There were individuals such as Dylan Thomas, of course. But what was really going on in regional poetry did not become apparent until a certain duality was observed, and it was most clearly to be seen in the oppositions of what might be called the poetry of the academy and the poetry of Pop.

One way to see this is to reflect that from the mid-1950s to the mid-1960s, while various gatherings and agendas were clustering around London periodicals (*Agenda,* for instance, begun by William Cookson and Peter Dale), the Pop poets were taking a more direct, often whimsical stance on writing, bypassing studied technique and allowing feeling and observation to adhere to the local or provincial imperative. This alternative had affinities with the folk tradition and sometimes linked with either protest movements or local groupings fired by linguistic difference, but essentially the "Pop" voice was in line with the nature of American popular music and the poetry of the Beats. In the late 1950s, for instance, before his emergence as a "Liverpool poet," Roger McGough was at university in Hull, learning predominantly from both

Philip Larkin and Christopher Logue. The only notable "literary" presence in his early work was a slight affinity with some French surrealism,
but it was the appeal of American low-key wit mixed with Logue's
reading that made an impact on him.[2]

By the early 1960s, the Movement had spawned a range of influential
voices, notably from the New Lines anthology of 1956; the poets coming in the wake of this, such as Amis and Larkin, saw the importance of
the demotic and the direct, but the literary antecedents are visible; there
is still something of the study there, despite their aim to give "a con-
certed reaction against the tangled and pretentious neo-Romanticism of
the post-war years."[3]

All this established literary history omits the fragmentary and indefinable individualists, and here the sense of persisting with a regional
stance is marked. The diversity is equally there: such figures as George
Mackay Brown in Orkney, Norman Nicholson in the Lakes, McGough,
Patten, and Henri in Liverpool, Heaney in Derry, and Dunn's first
collection, *Terry Street*, set in Hull. The regions were still mentally
distant, and just as elusive in the poetry of these years as in the fiction.
Where Barstow and Sillitoe sought to create representative sensibilities
against the status quo, the regional writers still maintained the rooted
tradition of moving from the particular to the universal. Three collections may be chosen to represent this: R. S. Thomas's *The Bread of
Truth* (1963), Seamus Heaney's *Death of a Naturalist* (1966), and *The
Mersey Sound* (1967).

These three books have many things in common, despite their very
different origins and cultural settings. They each, in different ways,
sustain an interest in the interminglings of language, the physical environment, and history as the composite definition of belonging. R. S.
Thomas sums it up in his poem, "Welsh" in which he embodies many of
the irrational attitudes formed either by overt nationalistic feelings or by
political resentments. The poem pinpoints a certain illogical dislike of
foreigners but also locates something brash and intrusive about the
English in Wales: an expression cognate with the daubed English place-
names and road-signs prevalent in large areas of Wales in the 1960s and
1970s, when Plaid Cymru were notably active and the aftermath of the
Investiture of the Prince of Wales in 1969 affected the nationalist stance.
Thomas knows the cultural force of ambivalent statements, but the
poem proves that he also appreciates the power of irony and the seeming
direct hatred of the bold words in short poetic lines.[4]

But Thomas sees place, the place on the periphery, as a purgatory also: a place "where you might have been sent / To learn patience" ("Country Cures"). Anyone visiting Wales must "stop at the bar" of speech; Thomas's earlier work had already established a dour, critical view of the Welsh people on the land. His invention of "Iago Prytherch" and "Cynddylan on a Tractor" still have the effect of giving a potent ambiguity to his anti-pastoral vision, being not too far away ideologically from Hanley or Evans. But Thomas sees another quality in his vision of Wales. As a priest with a parish in this isolated place, his own sense of being removed, aloof, is a way of enhancing and deepening his annotations of the isolation within and without. In "service," for instance, "We stand looking at each other / I take the word 'prayer' / and present it to them / I wait idly / wondering what their lips will / make of it."

When Thomas sees the hill farmers, he sees the hardness, the single-minded life entrapped in routine, with men ploughing "like slaves." The ultimate perception is one of apparent despair about Wales as a "fallen" land, as in the poem "A Country," the first half of which reflects on the imaginative distance his concept of "Wales" has gone from him. Then he denies the special status, the man-given nomenclature, and he sees just earth and rock: "It lay like a bone / thrown aside and of no use / for anything except shame to gnaw." In other words, central to Thomas's invention of his "Wales" is in many ways his ambiguity about its own myth when confronted by a tough, life-denying version of life, which appears like a limbo. This is often seen as a perpetual state of becoming and never actually being anything.

Whereas Dylan Thomas, in finding similar ambiguities in his stories of rural Pembroke, insisted on the surreal or the poetry of the bland and perfunctory life on the land enriched with human vibrancy, R. S. Thomas sees belonging as a two-edged sword of emotional uncertainty.

In Seamus Heaney's first collection, *Death of a Naturalist*, we have a collection that is arguably an exemplary template of the regional text as a fusion of language and identity tied to the land, to history, and to familial positionings. In these poems it is possible to find vestigial Wordsworthian insights, but, more profoundly, Heaney asserts that language itself, with its progeny of imaginative generation of meaning, creates the sense of place. Where Thomas sees a ploughman in a landscape, Heaney sees his father before him, "His shoulders globed like a full sail strung / between the shafts and the furrow."[5]

How does the writer, the individual, finally construct the patterns of emotions that make the sense of regional belonging? Heaney, in "At a Potato Digging," encapsulates the often complex answer in a memory-capture embracing at once historical inheritance and the immediacy of the sensual comprehension of land and self-identity inherent in that process of "making." Heaney's recurrent interest in the nature of the poet as a "makar" was there from the start, explained to the reader by means of showing the actions of absorbing place through sounds and attempts at naming, so crucial to the invention of a place. His poem "Centuries" succeeds in coalescing the historical resonance of reference with the Great Famine of the 1840s, while at the same time asserting the quasi-sacred nature of the earth and the allegiances to the land of the "peasant"—a word loaded throughout Irish history and indeed one subjected to a semantic shift of considerable importance. The poem locates a duality of identity in the farming people, at once intensely local and yet made notably significant through the vestiges of historical memory.[6]

When Heaney invokes the Great Famine of the 1840s, he simultaneously defines closeness to place and the intractability of historical process. The "live skulls, blind-eyed" image provides a hard empathic transference of earth to people. A regional awareness, then, is for Heaney a matter of words meeting intimately with things. His poetry delights in squeezing matter from names and sounds.

The poems in this first collection contain this fascination with the imagery of voice and speech, as developed more fully in the later collection, *North* (1975), in lines such as "The air was thick with a bass chorus" (*Death of a Naturalist*) or water in "Waterfall": "swallowed up / And regurgitated through this long throat." As the layers of physical and sensual description enrich the feeling of the specificity of place, Heaney intersperses the more directly human presence with the geological and physiological in poems like "Docker" and "Mid-Term Break."

As Heaney says in his essay, *The Governance of the Tongue* (the T. S. Eliot Memorial Lecture for 1986): "The poet is credited with a power to open unexpected and unedited communications between our nature and the nature of the reality we inhabit."[7] Heaney has always stressed the importance of poetry that vindicates its own inventiveness: for him it is an art tied to place and identity at the same time, and in his early poems in particular (up to the *North* collection), he was always in the mood to monitor his own progress toward the certainty of trusting "the nubbed treasure" of the immediate subject. The subject is, on the surface, the people, history, and landscape of Ireland; but Heaney has achieved what most exceptional regional writers achieve: the creative visualization of the mechanics of the self finding its validity and authentic meanings in a specific place. "A Local Habitation"—Shakespeare's phrase—was used as a title of a collection by Norman Nicholson in 1972, and in it he, like Heaney, attempts to fuse the intensely local with the infinite and perceptions of time and being. The two poets present an informative contrast, as Nicholson, accepting the power of a known community as a sustenance for a personal aesthetic, overtly asserts and celebrates a regional sensitivity; he even states, in a poem called "Have You Been to London?" that he is enriched by "A world left cold and draughty / unlatched, undone / by all the little illiterate boys / who hadn't been to London." He writes of Millom and Windscale in a forthright social commentary, marking his distance from the modern wherever possible. For Heaney, his Derry is part of a "ministry of fear" centered on London, as Ireland is reinforced as a segment of a postcolonial world. As with all concepts of "regional" and "national," when they interfuse, the results are creative, leading to a revisiting of what should be perfunctory but is, to a poet, a world waiting to be revealed anew. Hence, Heaney's early poetry is searching for a sense of the numinous in place. Nicholson stays outside, describing a world of hard knocks and self-making.

Death of a Naturalist, then, in the context of the 1960s, simultaneously opened up a fresh way of understanding the search for self-identity within such a weight of history, even when executed with a quasi-Wordsworthian sensibility. But Heaney's immersion in the vernacular of Ulster, together with his absorption of Anglo-Saxon and the sagas in his studies at Queen's, Belfast, moved from early uncertainties about how poetry could comprehend such massive historical and linguistic concepts to the writer of poems with a surface simplicity above rich layers of meanings and dualities.

In contrast, one of the most useful places to look for the relation of Pop poetry to regional awareness is in the "Mersey Sound" writing of Roger McGough, Brian Patten, and Adrian Henri. The momentous volume indicative of their achievement is *Penguin Modern Poets 10* (1967). In these poems, Liverpool as a landscape and Liverpool as a collection of people and provincial conditions mix to create an impressionistic account of a city at the center of a certain confidence of importance, at the point when the Beatles had emerged as a supergroup and, in terms of poetry and other writing, the city attained the status of model for a general renewal of interest in regional writing. As Patten was working as a reporter in Bootle and producing his small magazine, *Underdog*, with an eye toward America and the Beats, Sillitoe was writing a critique of the provincial mind in a new world of imminent mass-media dominance. Henri, an artist as well as a writer, had been exposed to continental influence in his interest in, for example, the Belgian painter, James Ensor, and the *Ubu Roi* plays of Alfred Jarry. But all this cosmopolitan influence was subsumed into a preoccupation with Liverpool.

All this is explained in Edward Lucie-Smith's book, *The Liverpool Scene* (1967), produced at the time of the "Mersey Sound" to capitalize on the city where it was all "happening." Lucie-Smith's photographs and neat captions beneath images of McGough and friends in a coffee bar or Henri dressed as Ubu make it clear that the erosion of class difference in local art was a potential revolution for English society. For example, in one sound bite, McGough says: "In Liverpool you're a poet one minute but the next minute you're talking about football, or you're buying bus tickets, or someone's kicking your head in down at the Blue Angel."[8]

Liverpool certainly has always been thought of as a remote place—somehow "beyond Lancashire." As McGough wrote recently in an article on his native city: "The thing about Liverpool is that we live in a city that looks out to the sea, and we feel cut off by land. If you take the East Lancs road out towards Manchester, it is not long before 'Our Tribe' quite suddenly ends. There is no transition. The accent, attitude, the loyalties, the sense of belonging stop abruptly."[9]

The poems in *The Mersey Sound* volume intermix personal humor with social commentary; they both describe a culture and send it up. They also introduce major themes and macrocosmic history so deftly that it is easy to overlook the sense of a subtext here in which ambivalence could topple into a certain cruel stance on the subjects, but everything is redeemed by a genuine sense of attachment to place and people, even when the landscape is, on the surface, potentially a "wasteland" and as mundane as Billy Casper's estate. The poems in the book include references to Woolworth, Batman, a bus conductor, breakfast cereal, a motorway, a girl with a hare-lip—that is, what is downbeat and ordinary, normally avoided or unnoticed, takes center stage. But the attraction and impact of these poems at the time is partly explained by the

juxtaposition of actual places in the Liverpool context with styles associated with a more European tradition, as in his use of the startling
personifications of surrealism, placing figures from elemental visions in
the mundane settings of Liverpool streets. This use of the obvious
landmarks, such as street names and cathedrals, placed with dissonance
by the side of an assertion of neo-Wordsworthian innocence, has a
startling impact. Like Patten, Henri can reach his stylistic effects without stretching beyond the diction of the everyday, the street, the bar. The
demotic in the case of Liverpool writing in this context is also the
universal, with thanks to the new pop lyrics of the decade.[10]

The ingredient that differentiates *The Mersey Sound* as a landmark
regional text, however, is the purposeful inclusion of locality by means
of fun, parody, ambiguity, and pastiche. The quintessential exponent of
this is McGough, who even wrote a short novel, *Frink, a Life in the Day
of* (1967), told around movements in the streets and flats of the city,
with meticulous in-jokes and typographical devices to maintain the
jokes and local humor. In his poem "Let Me Die a Youngman's Death,"
McGough includes lines that attain similar effects to those of Henri, but
McGough's are closer to song. The notion of the modern troubadour
seems to fit his work. In some of the best-known poems he appropriates
the modes of medieval sensual love poems such as those by Dafydd ap
Gwilym or François Villon in bringing together the modern context and
the bohemian, whimsical assertions of life so rich in his work.[11]

The reference to the Cavern is entirely typical of the spirit of the
performance scene at the time in student clubs and cafes. The humor of
the group The Scaffold, with their hit *Lily the Pink,* again maximizes the
local reference.

In *The Mersey Sound* it is possible to see the beginnings of what is
now the crossover art of poetry/stand-up comedy, and although
McGough does not really like the term "performance poet," it has to be
said that the work of the Liverpool poets in the 1960s made it possible to
write about place and local belonging with modes and attitudes other
than the Georgian or the Larkinesque. Elegy was not the only option.

Grevel Lindop points out that there are other reasons for the success
of what might be called "Underground" poetry in this Liverpool context. He points out the tendency of these writers to "use a rather porten-
tous style for the treatment of comically insignificant or undignified
subjects," and he notes Brian Patten's poem, "Maud, 1965" as an example. Lindop notes: "An appreciation of the poem depends upon an

instinctive understanding on the part of the audience of the way in which the poet is flouting traditional decorum."[12] This is crucially important to an understanding of the significance of how these poets depicted and indeed recreated their locality: they knew the audience. How many modern poets can say that they began their writing careers with a clear sense of audience and a regular acquaintance with those same people within a local culture? In this sense, the Mersey poets are closer to the Victorian dialect poets of the regional reading circuits and literary clubs than to the normal twentieth-century milieu for the production of poetry.

Even the marketing of the Mersey poets indicates this sense of closeness to locality and audience, shown in the carefully posed images on the covers of their collections, the studied dress and quotes in Lucie-Smith's book, and even a blurb such as this on the cover of McGough's *Frink*:

Roger McGough was born in Liverpool in 1937, when the November lay on the ground. ... After teaching for three years joined up with John Gorman and Michael McGear to form the Scaffold humour group. Although now a full-time writer and performer still enjoys being a very part-time lecturer in Liberal Studies at Liverpool College of Art.[13]

The Mersey Sound and the associated mediation of the new Pop or Underground poetry provided a new model for writing about locality: it cut across class boundaries, exploited the whole idea of a known audience, and took away much of the distance and mystique attached to the notion of the "writer" in English society. It was the age of television, and McGough extended this subject area and humor into drama and sketches. The breaking-down of genres and the cultural definition of poetry as a highbrow art were on the way out.

Each in very different ways, then, Heaney, R. S. Thomas, and the Mersey poets represent some of the prominent varieties of regional poetry in these years. Reference to "national" or "postcolonial" concepts and commentary has been omitted largely from the discussion; yet, in an ironic way, these writers from such polarities of regional consciousness may be, arguably, representative also of the tendency of each generation to reinvent its vision of what constitutes regional belonging. Whether they have ultimately given a more genuine picture of regional consciousness than, say, popular fiction, such as sagas, is open to debate. But the debate will always have to contend with mechanisms in creativity that deal with breaking with the familiar, with making the "stone stony," as the Russian formalists might argue. Only by making us look at the familiar through inventive and startling points of view have these poets shocked readers into considering that peripheral state of being denigrated by Matthew Arnold: a cultural–historical factor that may always have a bearing on how we construct regional belonging in Britain.[14]

Conclusions

This survey has moved from a focus on the invention of region as a place in the mind to the Modern/Postmodern modes of seeing "region" as something either outdated or no longer important. In Barry Hines's *A Kestrel for a Knave*, the setting is given as something marginal even in terms of Yorkshire or a place that is vaguely "north." But this is entirely typical of what has happened to the concept of place in the modern consciousness. Globalization and uniformity, the insidious dangers for culture of the encroaching sameness of every place—these are detrimental to that traditional British power in the arts of imagining a place as different, special, and having qualities of value to anyone.

As discussed in the Introduction, the literary history here has stayed clear of the muddle that is "national" as opposed to "regional," but what has become clear in the process of examining some of the key works in the regional tradition is that certain aspects of community in all the varieties of British culture, from Orkney to Cornwall and from Dublin to Anglesey—if we use "British" to mean "of the British Isles" (and this has been my sense in this book)—remain constant. These are a repeatedly important need to know a place with boundaries, definitions, and moral structures, a desire to express a special local quality traditionally known as "character," and a value placed on the provincial mind.

The axis of center/periphery, so important for Matthew Arnold when he looked at Celtic literature and culture and compared "philistine" nature with classical, has always had a loaded perspective—one that sees class and education as formative instruments of change and stability—hence the recurrent theme of escape and exile in regional writing

From Edgeworth's *Castle Rackrent* (1800) to Heaney's *Death of a Naturalist* (1966), there has been a fascination with the confrontation of the need for home and the pull of elsewhere. Even in the eighteenth century, the attraction of London for a talented or ambitious young person (such as James Boswell, whose father considered the Borders to be enough for anyone) has always been linked to glamour as much as to career or ambition, so it is not surprising that certain themes in regional writing persist. The most common of these is the meditation of place and belonging in the tourist and heritage-industry brochures, and it is clear that certain writers—Burns in Ayrshire, Wordsworth in the Lakes, and so on—will always be "sold" and interpreted as having claimed a certain geographical and ideological area for their own.

This survey has noted the diversity and the similarities across the length and breadth of the islands. I hope that the works discussed have reminded readers that a writer with a "region" as imaginative sustenance cannot escape the entrenched concepts of family, affections, love of place, language, and geomorphology. Of all these aspects, the preceding pages have stressed that language is instrumental here, and that of all the potentially interesting organizing principles in these writings, language is the dominant one. In writers as different as Synge, Burnley, Grassic Gibbon, Heaney, and Barstow, it is what ultimately represents a specific place and people.

The environmental perspective has remained also—and as Larkin's poem, "Here," reinforces—a place on the cultural and mental periphery has a particularly ambiguous attraction for a writer. He manages to convey the mixed senses of belonging and estrangement, as if some Frankenstein-created figure is seeing a landscape for the first time; but Larkin also layers description and gives the diction a rich sensuality, deftly relating a sense of identity to the quiet, unchanging place.[1] It is a sense of place as an enforced retreat, an isolation somehow against the perplexities of modernity. The isolation "clarifies."

Therefore, at the center of the discussion there will always be the issue of what happens if we continue to denationalize our regional sense. There will always be writers like Patrick Kavanagh, who wish to dissent from what he called the "myth of Ireland as a spiritual entity."[2] As a polar opposite, there is a strong argument to suggest that Richard

Hoggart's view of a collective, known microcosmic community will always be there as a counterideology to global sharing and uniformity.

Finally, it has to be acknowledged that a concept such as "regional" could be shifted to urban writing with no real change of thematic interest, as Arthur Morrison's stories show; even in Dickens, a largely metropolitan writer, we have a regional writer if we omit the metropolitan context and read his London as a place of the mind more than a geographical entity. In fact, the ways in which the domestic and the rural—like Wemmick's castle in *Great Expectations* or Peggotty's coastline in *David Copperfield*—participate in Dickens sets up binary oppositions that are just as powerful as anything rather more purposefully attempted in, for instance, Hardy's fiction, where symbolic instruments of modernity crush the traditional, the rural, and the small-scale.

In specifically English writing, a cursory look at the contemporary poetry scene suggests that the Georgian modes will not easily disappear, and in fiction regional popular fiction is as strong as ever in the publishers' lists. The current British bestseller lists (2002) contain four regional novels, set in Wales, Yorkshire, the Lakes, and Liverpool. What they all have in common is that they are set in the period between 1939 and 1959. Until popular fiction ceases to be caught in certain market-led stereotypical and invented places of the mind, innovative regional writing will continue to come from writers who start from a different standpoint, such as W. G. Sebald in Norfolk and Suffolk, who has used layers of European historical reference mixed with an intense association with an adopted homeland.

Ultimately, I hope this rather selective work of literary history has opened up some fresh thinking on what we have seen, and will continue to see, as a "regional" work in Britain. There will inevitably have been omissions, but it is hoped that some works—such as Hanley's—have been retrieved from the forgotten byways of literary history and that critics and historians will continue to explore this rich body of work.

Notes

Introduction

1. See Asa Briggs, *Victorian Cities* (London: Penguin, 1963), pp. 59–60.

2. From a Radio 3 discussion on Stevenson, 14 October 2000.

3. See the essay by Trevor R. Pringle, "The Privation of History: Landseer, Victoria and the Highland Myth," in Denis Cosgrove and Stephen Daniels (eds.), *The Iconography of Landscape* (Cambridge: Cambridge University Press, 1988), pp. 119–141.

4. Arnold Bennett, *A Man from the North* (Stroud, U.K.: Sutton, 1994), p. 1.

5. William Shakespeare, *As You Like It,* Act I, Scene 1, ll. 113–119.

6. See Patrick Joyce, *Democratic Subjects* (Cambridge: Cambridge University Press, 1994), pp. 41–47.

7. A. J. P. Taylor, *English History 1914–1945* (London: Penguin, 1975), p. 221.

8. Phyllis Bentley, *The English Regional Novel* (London: Allen and Unwin, 1941), p. 8.

9. See *Fact,* July 1937, p. 6.

10. John Lucas, *England and Englishness* (London: Hogarth, 1990), p. 133.

11. See Donald Read, *The English Provinces c. 1760–1960* (Edward Arnold, 1964), p. 263.

Chapter 1

1. Ronald Blythe, *Talking about John Clare* (Nottingham, U.K.: Trent Books, 1999), p. 12.

2. Peter Burke, *Popular Culture in Early Modern Europe* (London: Wildwood, 1988), p. 12.

3. See Mikhail Bakhtin, *The Dialogic Imagination* (Houston, TX: University of Texas Press, 1981), pp. 84– 85; see also Simon Trezise's longer discussion in *The West Country as a Literary Invention* (Exeter, U.K.: University of Exeter Press, 2000), pp. 139–171.

4. Simon Trezise, "Places in Time: Discovering the Chronotope in *Tess of the D'Urbervilles,*" *Critical Survey,* 5, no. 2 (1993): 137.

5. R. D. Blackmore, *Lorna Doone* (Oxford: Oxford University Press, 1925), p. 2.

6. Declan Kiberd, "Irish Literature and Irish History," in R. F. Foster (ed.), *The Oxford History of Ireland* (Oxford: Oxford University Press, 1989), p. 263.

7. See Burke, *Popular Culture*, p. 12.

Chapter 2

1. See John Sutherland's entry on regional fiction in *The Macmillan Guide to Victorian Fiction* (London: Macmillan, 1980).

2. Charles Lamb, *Essays of Elia* (London: Odhams, 1910), p. 109.

3. Elizabeth Gaskell, *Cranford* (London: Penguin, 1986), p. 53.

4. Ibid., p. 41.

5. See Peter Keating, *The Haunted Study* (London: Secker and Warburg, 1989), p. 331.

6. John Clare, "The Lamentations of Round Oak Water," in Merryn Williams and Raymond Williams (eds.), *John Clare: Selected Poetry and Prose* (London: Methuen, 1986), p. 39.

7. See Joyce, *Democratic Subjects*, p. 76.

8. Raymond Williams, *Writing in Society* (Cambridge: Verso, 1989), p. 234.

9. Elizabeth Gaskell, *North and South* (London: Penguin, 1970), p. 96.

10. Ibid., p. 102.

11. Ibid., p. 108.

12. Ibid., p. 259.

13. Ibid., p. 144.

14. Elizabeth Gaskell, *The Life of Charlotte Brontë* (London: Dent, 1908), p. 11.

15. Emily Brontë, *Wuthering Heights* (London: Penguin, 1975), p. 57.

16. Lucasta Miller, *The Brontë Myth* (London: Vintage, 2001), p. 201.

17. John Hewish, *Emily Brontë: A Critical and Biographical Study* (London: Macmillan, 1969), p. 120.

18. Brontë, *Wuthering Heights*, p. 46.

19. Ibid.

20. Gaskell, *Life of Charlotte Brontë*, p. 13.

21. See interview with Roy Foster, *The Guardian*.

22. Declan Kiberd, "Irish Literature and Irish History," pp. 259–260.

23. Ibid., p. 261.

24. Samuel Lover, *Handy Andy* (London: W. Nicholson, 1842), p. 1.

25. Hedge school: in Ireland, an outdoor school held in the shelter of a hedge.

26. Declan Kiberd, "Confronting Famine: Carelton's Peasantry," in *Irish Classics* (London: Granta, 2000), p. 269.

27. William Carleton, *Traits and Stories of the Irish Peasantry, Vol. 1* (Gerrard's Cross, U.K.: Colin Smythe, 1990), p. i.

28. Ibid., p. iii.

29. Ibid., p. xxiv.

30. Kiberd, "Confronting Famine," p. 268.

31. Carleton, *Traits and Stories of the Irish Peasantry*, pp. 265–266.

32. Lover, *Handy Andy*, p. 47.

33. See Prys Morgan, "From a Death to a View: The Hunt for the Welsh Past in the Romantic Period," in Eric Hobsbawn and Terence Ranger (eds.), *The Invention of Tradition* (Cambridge: Canto, 1983).

34. Ibid., p. 60.

35. Roland Mathias, *Anglo–Welsh Literature: An Illustrated History* (Cardiff: Poetry Wales Press, 1987), p. 65.

36. See Morgan, "From a Death to a View," p. 80.

37. George Borrow, *Wild Wales* (London: Collins, 1955), p. 75.

38. Thomas Gray, "The Bard," in Arthur Johnston (ed.), *Selected Poems of Gray and Collins* (London: Arnold, 1967), p. 86, ll. 125–127.

Chapter 3

1. Thomas Hardy, *Far from the Madding Crowd* (London: Marshall Cavendish, 1991), p. 48.

2. See Raymond Chapman, "A True Representation: Speech in the Novels of Thomas Hardy," in Beatrice White (ed.), *Essays and Studies* (London: John Murray, 1983), pp. 40–55.

3. Ibid., p. 41.

4. Ibid., p. 55.

5. Hardy, *Far from the Madding Crowd*, p. 52.

6. See Robert Gittings, *Young Thomas Hardy* (London: Penguin, 1978), pp. 258–259.

7. Chapman, "A True Representation," p. 54.

8. Georgina Boyes, *The Imagined Village* (Manchester, U.K.: Manchester University Press, 1993), p. 29.

9. Trezise, *West Country*, p. 21.

10. Blackmore, *Lorna Doone*, p. 108.

11. Trezise, *West Country*, p. 136.

12. Blackmore, *Lorna Doone*, p. 53.

13. See Margaret Drabble, *Arnold Bennett* (London: Weidenfeld and Nicholson, 1974), pp. 2–3.

14. See Frank Swinnerton, "Introduction," in Arnold Bennett, *Anna of the Five Towns* (London: Penguin, 1954), p. 12.

15. William Shakespeare, *The Taming of the Shrew,* Act I, Scene 2, ll. 48–50.

16. Arnold Bennett, *Anna of the Five Towns* (London: Penguin, 1954), p. 79.

17. Ibid., p. 98.

18. Ibid., p. 29.

19. Ibid., p. 39.

20. Ibid., p. 48.

21. See Ian Maxwell, "Highland Clearances," *Family History,* 72 (September 2001): 29.

22. *Literature*, 48 (17 September 1898): 1.

23. Andrew Birkin, *J. M. Barrie and the Lost Boys* (London: Batsford, 1988).

24. J. M. Barrie, *Margaret Ogilvy* (London: Hodder and Stoughton, 1897), p. 88.

25. S. R. Crockett, *Cleg Kelly* (London: Smith, Elder, 1896), p. 79.

26. T. M. Devine, *The Scottish Nation 1700–2000* (London: Penguin, 2000), p. 297.

Chapter 4

1. See Helen Jewell, *The North–South Divide* (Manchester, U.K.: Manchester University Press, 1994); also Keith Robbins, "North and South Then and Now," *History Today*, 38 (April 1988), pp. 23–28. Both texts discuss the nature of the definitions of "north."

2. Iain Chambers, *Border Dialogues* (London: Routledge, 1990), p. 53.

3. Michael Wheeler, *English Fiction of the Victorian Period* (London: Longmans, 1985), pp. 156–157.

4. John Thomson, *Francis Thompson the Preston-Born Poet* (London: Simkin-Marshall, 1912).

5. Robin Young, "At the Margins: Outsider Figures in Nineteenth-Century Poetry," in H. W. Ludwig and L. Fietz (eds.), *Poetry in the British Isles: Non-Metropolitan Perspectives* (Cardiff: University of Wales Press, 1995), p. 31.

6. Edward Thomas, *A Language Not to Be Betrayed* (Manchester, U.K.: Carcanet, 1981), p. 200.

7. Bennett, *Man from the North*, pp. 42–43.

8. Briggs, *Victorian Cities*, p. 143.

9. W. Riley, *Sunset Reflections* (London: Herbert Jenkins, 1957), p. 57.

10. Peter Holdsworth, *The Rebel Tyke: Bradford and J. B. Priestley* (Bradford, U.K.: Bradford Libraries, 1994), p. 19.

11. See William Andrews, introduction to Burnley's poetry, in Charles H. Forshaw (ed.), *The Poets of Keighley, Bingley and Howarth* (Bradford, U.K.: Thornton and Pearson, 1891), pp. 42–43.

12. See an account of the bookman's life in John Gross, *The Rise and Fall of the Man of Letters* (London: Penguin, 1977), particularly chapter 7.

13. James Burnley, *Literary Reflections of Bradford 1870–1890* (ms. held in Bradford Central Library literary manuscript collection).

14. Ibid.

15. Ibid.

16. Forshaw, *Poets of Keighley, Bingley and Howarth*, p. 84.

17. James Burnley, *West Riding Sketches* (London: Hodder and Stoughton, 1875), p. 11.

18. Burnley, *Literary Reflections of Bradford*.

19. F. Legouis & L. Cazamian, *A History of English Literature* (London: Dent, 1967), p. 1324.

20. Elizabeth Gaskell, *Mary Barton* (London: Penguin, 1988), p. 100.

21. Arthur Morrison, *Tales of Mean Streets* (London: Academy Press, 1967), p. 22; see also the discussion about Clara getting a job in chapter 3, George Gissing, *The Nether World* (Oxford: Oxford University Press, 1992), pp. 26–27.

22. See Margot Norris, "The Lethal Turn of the Twentieth Century," in Robert Newman (ed.), *Centuries, Ends, Narratives, Means* (Cambridge: Cambridge University Press, 1998), pp. 151–159.

23. Morrison, *Tales of Mean Streets*, p. 29.

24. Lewis C. Roberts, "Disciplining and Disinfecting Working-Class Readers in the Victorian Public Library," *Victorian Literature and Culture*, 26 (1998): 106.

25. Morrison, *Tales of Mean Streets*, p. 16.

26. Ibid., p. 36.

27. John Hartley, *The Clock Almanac* [for 1899] (Bradford, U.K.: W. Nicholson, 1899), p. 44.

28. Somerset Maugham, *Liza of Lambeth* (London: Heinemann, 1948), p. 4.

29. Morrison, *Tales of Mean Streets*, p. 29.

30. Textual references are to Christopher Ricks's edition of *A Shropshire Lad* (London: Penguin, 1989).

31. Maxwell Fraser, *Companion to Worcestershire* (London: Methuen, 1939), p. 221.

32. Briggs, *Victorian Cities*, p. 31.

33. Barrie Trinder, *A History of Shropshire* (London: Phillimore, 1983), p. 100.

34. Richard Perceval Graves, *A. E. Housman, the Scholar–Poet* (London: Routledge, 1979), p. 48.

35. A. E. Housman, "The Name and Nature of Poetry," in Christopher Ricks (ed.), *A. E. Housman, Collected Poems and Prose* (London: Penguin, 1989), p. 352.

36. Thomas Hardy, *Tess of the D'Urbervilles* (London: Penguin, 1978), p. 61.

Chapter 5

1. E. M. Forster, *Howard's End* (London: Penguin, 1973), p. 127.

2. T. S. Eliot, "The Waste Land," in *Collected Poems* (London: Faber, 1963), p. 65.

3. Ibid., p. 72.

4. James Joyce, "A Little Cloud," in *Dubliners* (London: Penguin, 1969), p. 401.

5. Edward Thomas, "Adlestrop," in *Selected Poems* (London: Faber, 1964), p. 48.

6. Ibid., p. 32.

7. T. R. Henn, "Introduction," in *J. M. Synge: The Complete Plays* (London: Methuen, 1981), p. 6.

8. J. M. Synge, "Preface," in *Playboy of the Western World* (London: Methuen, 1981), p. 174.

9. Ibid., p. 174.

10. Ibid., p. 188.

11. Ibid., p. 218.

12. T. R. Henn, "Introduction," p. 12.

13. George Douglas Brown, *The House with the Green Shutters* (Edinburgh: Canongate, 1999), p. 184.

14. Ibid., p. 128.

15. Ibid., p. 129.

16. Ibid., p. 129.

17. D. H. Lawrence, "You Touched Me," in *Selected Tales* (London: Heinemann, 1982), p. 132.

18. Brown, *The House with the Green Shutters*, p. 18.

19. See John Harris, "Introduction," in Caradoc Evans, *My People* (Bridgend, U.K.: Seren, 1997), pp. 35–37.

20. Ibid., p. 39.

21. Edward Thomas, *Wales* (London: A. C. Black, 1905), p. 25.

22. Evans, *My People*, p. 68.

23. D. H. Lawrence, "Nottingham and the Mining Country," in *Selected Essays* (London: Penguin, 1950), p. 119.

Chapter 6

1. Hugh MacDiarmid, "A Drunk Man Looks at a Thistle," in *Selected Poems* (London: Penguin, 1992), p. 34.

2. Ibid., p. 39.

3. Alan Bold, *MacDiarmid: The Terrible Crystal* (London: Routledge, 1983), p. 55.

4. D. H. Lawrence, *Sons and Lovers* (London: Penguin, 1983), p. 19.

5. Ibid., p. 143.

6. D. H. Lawrence, *Women in Love* (London: Penguin, 1989), p. 298.

7. Lawrence, "Nottingham and the Mining Country," p. 118.

8. Valentine Cunningham, *British Writers of the Thirties* (Oxford: Oxford University Press, 1989), p. 329.

9. J. B. Priestley, *English Journey* (London: Mandarin, 1994), p. 204.

10. Ibid., p. 51.

11. Ibid., p. 51.

12. Bentley, *English Regional Novel*, p. 8.

13. Arthur Calder-Marshall, "Fiction," *Fact,* 15 July 1937, pp. 39–40.

14. George Orwell, "Literature and the Left," in *The Collected Essays, Journalism and Letters 1942–3* (London: Penguin,1970), pp. 334–337.

15. George Orwell, *Coming Up for Air* (London: Penguin, 1981), p. 43.

16. Ibid., p. 74.

17. B. L. Coombes, *Miner's Day* (London: Penguin, 1945), p. 62.

18. Ibid., p. 30.

19. Winifred Holtby, *South Riding* (London: Virago, 1988), p. 40.

20. Phyllis Bentley, "Yorkshire and the Novelist," in *Essays by Divers Hands* (London: Oxford University Press, 1965), p. 152.

21. See Phyllis Bentley, *O Dreams, O Destinations* (London: Gollancz, 1962), in particular chapter 14.

22. Winifred Holtby, *South Riding*, p. 47.

23. Ibid., pp. 46–47.

24. Ibid., pp. 25–26.

25. Ibid., p. 31.

26. Philip Larkin, "The Whitsun Weddings," in *Collected Poems* (London: Faber, 1988), p. 116.

27. See Flora Thompson, *Lark Rise to Candleford* (Oxford: Oxford University Press, 1945), chapter 5.

28. Ibid., p. 98.

29. See J. B. Pick, "Introduction," in Neil Gunn, *The Key of the Chest* (Edinburgh: Canongate), p. v.

30. See Tom Crawford, "Introduction," in Lewis Grassic Gibbon, *A Scots Quair* (Edinburgh: Canongate, 1995), p. x.

31. Lewis Grassic Gibbon, *A Scots Quair* (Edinburgh: Canongate, 1995), p. 108.

32. Ibid., p. 32.

33. Ibid., p. 157.

33. Neil Gunn, *The Key of the Chest* (London: Faber & Faber, 1945).

Chapter 7

1. Elizabeth Berridge, "Notes from the Boilerhouse" *London Magazine* (December 1999): 51–62.

2. Ibid., p. 58.

3. Dylan Thomas, *Under Milk Wood: The Dylan Thomas Omnibus* (London: Phoenix, 1995), p. 341.

4. Raymond Garlick, *An Introduction to Anglo–Welsh Literature* (Cardiff: University of Wales Press, 1972), p. 10.

5. Unpublished interview, 1979.

6. Ibid.

7. Ibid.

8. John Harris, "Introduction," in Evans, *My People*, p. 9.

8. Ibid., p. 45.

9. Ibid., p. 108.

10. James Hanley, *The Welsh Sonata* (London: Verschoyle, 1957), p. 9.

11. T. R. Henn (ed.), *Synge: The Complete Plays* (London: Methuen, 1981), p. 19.

12. Ibid., p. 186.

13. Hanley, *Welsh Sonata*, p. 13.

14. Thomas, *Under Milk Wood*, p. 344.

15. Ibid., p. 357.

16. Hanley, *Welsh Sonata,* p. 44.

17. Ibid., p. 69.

18. Ibid., p. 25.

19. Ibid., p. 29.

20. The prevalence of deictic expressions throughout the novel indicates a distancing effect, intended perhaps to maintain the sense of the orality of the narrative.

21. Hanley, *Welsh Sonata*, p. 56.

22. Thomas, *Under Milk Wood*, p. 341.

23. Hanley, *Welsh Sonata,* p. 181.

24. Alan Ross (ed.), *James Hanley: The Last Voyage* (London: Harvill, 1997), p. x.

25. See David N. Thomas, "Under Milk Wood's Birth in Exile," *New Welsh Review*, 52 (2000): 49.

26. M. Wynn Thomas, *Corresponding Cultures* (Cardiff: University of Wales Press, 1999), p. 46.

Chapter 8

1. Richard Hoggart, *The Uses of Literacy* (London: Penguin, 1957), p. 33.

2. Bentley, *O Dreams, O Destinations*, p. 237.

3. Ibid., p. 266.

4. See J. B. Priestley, "Why Phyllis Bentley Could Not Retreat," *Yorkshire Post*, 19 November 1964, p. 6.

5. John Braine, *Room at the Top* (London: Penguin, 1959), p. 7.

6. Arnold Wesker, *Roots* (London: Longman, 1967), p. 69.

7. Randall Stevenson, *The British Novel since the Thirties* (London: Batsford, 1986), p. 124.

8. Braine, *Room at the Top*, p. 34.

9. Ibid., p. 86.

10. Ibid., p. 97.

11. Ibid., p. 97.

12. Barry Hines, *A Kestrel for a Knave* (London: Michael Joseph, 1974), p. 30.

13. Ibid., p. 68.

14. Ibid., p. 79.

15. Ibid., p. 79.

16. See Paul Barker, "Review of Stan Barstow, *In My Own Time,*" *Times Literary Supplement,* 11 January 2002, p. 32.

Chapter 9

1. A. Alvarez (ed.), *The New Poetry* (London: Penguin, 1962), p. 24.

2. See Stephen Wade, *Gladsongs and Gatherings* (Liverpool: Liverpool University Press, 2001), p. 7.

3. See Ian Hamilton, "The Making of the Movement," in M. Schmidt and Grevel Lindop (eds.), *British Poetry since 1960* (Manchester, U.K.: Carcanet, 1972), p. 70.

4. R. S. Thomas, "Welsh," in *Collected Poems 1945–1990* (London: Phoenix, 2000), p. 129.

5. Seamus Heaney, "Follower," in *Death of a Naturalist* (London: Faber, 1966), p. 24.

6. Ibid., p. 31.

7. Seamus Heaney, *The Governance of the Tongue* (London: Faber, 1988), p. 93.

8. See images in Edward Lucie-Smith, *The Liverpool Scene* (London: Carroll, 1967), pp. 30–33.

9. See Roger McGough, "We Are Proud to Be Scousers," *Daily Mail*, 2 October 1998, p. 11.

10. Adrian Henri, "Liverpool Poems," in *Penguin Modern Poets 10: The Mersey Sound* (London: Penguin, 1967), p. 16.

11. Roger McGough, "Let Me Die a Youngman's Death," in *Penguin Modern Poets,* p. 91.

12. Grevel Lindop, "Poetry, Rhetoric and the Mass Audience: The Case of the Liverpool Poets," in M. Schmidt & Grevel Lindop, *British Poetry since 1960*, p. 97.

13. See cover of Roger McGough, *Frink, A Life in the Day Of* (London: Michael Joseph, 1967).

14. See the discussion of Arnold in Hans-Werner Ludwig and Lothar Fietz, *Poetry in the British Isles: Non-Metropolitan Perspectives* (Cardiff: University of Wales Press, 1995), pp. 48–51.

Conclusions

1. Philip Larkin, "Here," in *Collected Poems* (London: Faber, 1988), p. 136.

2. See Antoinette Quinn (ed.), *Patrick Kavanagh: Selected Poems* (London: Penguin, 1996); Introduction, p. xxi.

Bibliography

Note: The first category refers to works cited in the discussions of texts. The second is for books consulted in wider reading. The citations for critical and historical discussions are for texts used. Dates of first editions have been incorporated into the text.

Primary Sources

Barrie, J. M. *Margaret Ogilvy by Her Son*. London: Hodder and Stoughton, 1897.

Barstow, Stan. *A Kind of Loving*. London: Hale, 2001.

Bennett, Arnold. *Anna of the Five Towns*. London: Penguin, 1954.

Bennett, Arnold. *A Man from the North*. Stroud, U.K.: Sutton, 1994.

Bentley, Phyllis. *O Dreams, O Destinations*. London: Gollancz, 1962.

Bentley, Phyllis. *The English Regional Novel*. London: Allen and Unwin, 1941.

Blackmore, R. D. *Lorna Doone*. Oxford: Oxford University Press 1925.

Borrow, George. *Wild Wales*. London: Collins, 1955.

Braine, John. *Room at the Top*. London: Penguin, 1959.

Brontë, Emily. *Wuthering Heights*. London: Penguin, 1975.

Brown, George Douglas. *The House with the Green Shutters*. Edinburgh: Canongate, 1999.

Burnley, James. *West Riding Sketches*. London: Hodder and Stoughton, 1875.

Carleton, William. *Traits and Stories of the Irish Peasantry*. Gerrard's Cross, U.K.: Colin Smythe, 1990.

Clare, John. *John Clare: Selected Poetry and Prose*. London: Methuen, 1986.

Coombes, B. L. *Miner's Day*. London: Penguin, 1945.

Crockett, S. R. *Cleg Kelly*. London: Smith Elder, 1896.

Eliot, T. S. *The Waste Land*. In *Collected Poems*. London: Faber, 1963.

Evans, Caradoc. *My People*. Bridgend, U.K.: Seren, 1997.

Forster, E. M. *Howard's End*. London: Penguin, 1973.

Gaskell, Elizabeth. *Cranford*. London: Penguin, 1986.

Gaskell, Elizabeth. *Mary Barton*. London: Penguin, 1988.

Gaskell, Elizabeth. *North and South*. London: Penguin, 1970.

Gaskell, Elizabeth. *The Life of Charlotte Brontë*. London: Dent, 1908.

Gibbon, Lewis Grassic. *A Scots Quair*. Edinburgh: Canongate, 1995.

Hanley, James. *The Welsh Sonata*. London: Verschoyle, 1957.

Hardy, Thomas. *Far from the Madding Crowd*. London: Marshall Cavendish, 1991.

Hardy, Thomas. *Tess of the D'Urbervilles*. London: Penguin, 1978.

Heaney, Seamus. *Death of a Naturalist*. London: Faber, 1966.

Heaney, Seamus. *The Governance of the Tongue*. London: Faber, 1988.

Hines, Barry. *A Kestrel for a Knave*. London: Michael Joseph, 1974.

Holtby, Winifred. *South Riding*. London: Virago, 1988.

Housman, A. E. *Selected Poetry and Prose*. London: Penguin, 1989.

Joyce, James. *Dubliners*. London: Penguin, 1969.

Larkin, Philip. *Collected Poems*. London: Faber, 1988.

Lawrence, D. H. *Selected Essays*. London: Penguin, 1950.

Lawrence, D. H. *Sons and Lovers*. London: Penguin, 1983.

Lawrence, D. H. *Women in Love*. London: Penguin, 1989.

Lover, Samuel. *Handy Andy*. London: W. Nicholson, 1842.

MacDiarmid, Hugh. *Selected Poems*. London: Penguin, 1992.

Maugham, Somerset. *Liza of Lambeth*. London: Heinemann, 1948.

McGough, Roger, Henri, Adrian, and Patten, Brian. *Penguin Modern Poets 10: The Mersey Sound*. London: Penguin, 1967.

Morrison, Arthur. *Tales of Mean Streets*. London: Academy Press, 1967.

Orwell, George. *Collected Essays, Journalism and Letters 1942–3*. London: Penguin, 1970.

Orwell, George. *Coming Up for Air*. London: Penguin, 1981.

Priestley, J. B. *English Journey*. London: Mandarin, 1994.

Synge, J. M. *The Playboy of the Western World*. London: Methuen, 1981.

Thomas, Dylan. *The Dylan Thomas Omnibus*. London: Phoenix, 1995.

Thomas, Edward. *A Language Not to Be Betrayed*. Manchester, U.K.: Carcanet, 1981.

Thomas, Edward. *Selected Poems*. London: Faber, 1964.

Thomas, R. S. *Collected Poems, 1945–90*. London: Phoenix, 2000.

Thompson, Flora. *Lark Rise to Candleford*. Oxford: Oxford University Press 1945.

Secondary Sources: Books

Alvarez, A. (ed.). *The New Poetry*. London: Penguin, 1962.

Bakhtin, Mikhail. *The Dialogic Imagination*. Houston, TX: University of Texas Press, 1981.

Birkin, Andrew. *J. M. Barrie and the Lost Boys*. London: Batsford, 1988.

Blythe, Ronald. *Talking about John Clare*. Nottingham, U.K.: Trent Books, 1999.

Bold, Alan. *MacDiarmid: The Terrible Crystal*. London: Routledge, 1983.

Boyes, Georgina. *The Imagined Village*. Manchester, U.K.: Manchester University Press, 1993.

Briggs, Asa. *Victorian Cities*. London: Penguin, 1963.

Chambers, Iain. *Border Dialogues*. London: Routledge, 1990.

Cosgrove, Denis, & Daniels, Stephen (eds.). *The Iconography of Landscape*. Cambridge: Cambridge University Press, 1988.

Cunningham, Valentine. *British Writers of the Thirties*. Oxford: Oxford University Press 1989.

Devine, T. M. *The Scottish Nation 1700–2000*. London: Penguin, 2000.

Drabble, Margaret. *Arnold Bennett*. London: Weidenfeld and Nicholson, 1974.

Forshaw, Charles, H. *The Poets of Keighley, Bingley and Howarth*. Bradford, U.K.: Thornton and Pearson, 1891.

Fraser, Maxwell. *Companion to Worcestershire*. London: Methuen, 1939.

Garlick, Raymond. *An Introduction to Anglo–Welsh Literature*. Cardiff: University of Wales Press, 1972.

Gittings, Robert. *Young Thomas Hardy*. London: Penguin, 1978.

Graves, Richard Perceval. *A. E. Housman, the Scholar–Poet*. London: Routledge, 1979.

Gross, John. *James Hanley: The Rise and Fall of the Man of Letters*. London: Penguin, 1977.

Hartley, John. *The Clock Almanac*. Bradford, U.K.: W. Nicholson, 1899.

Hobsbawn, Philip, and Ranger, Terence. *The Invention of Tradition*. Cambridge: Canto, 1983.

Holdsworth, Peter. *The Rebel Tyke: Bradford and J. B. Priestley*. Bradford, U.K.: Bradford Libraries, 1994.

Jewell, Helen. *The North–South Divide*. Manchester, U.K.: Manchester University Press, 1994.

Joyce, Patrick. *Democratic Subjects*. Manchester, U.K.: Manchester University Press, 1994.

Keating, Peter. *The Haunted Study*. London: Secker and Warburg, 1989.

Kiberd, Declan. *Irish Classics*. London: Granta, 2000.

Lamb, Charles. *Essays of Elia*. London: Odhams, 1910.

Legouis, F., and Cazamian, L. *A History of English Literature*. London: Dent, 1967.

Lucas, John. *England and Englishness*. London: Hogarth, 1990.

Mathias, Roland. *Anglo–Welsh Literature: An Illustrated History*. Cardiff: Poetry Wales Press, 1987.

Miller, Lucasta. *The Brontë Myth*. London: Vintage, 2001.

Quinn, Antoinette (ed.). *Patrick Kavanagh: Selected Poems*. London: Penguin, 1996.

Riley, W. *Sunset Reflections*. London: Herbert Jenkins, 1957.

Ross, Alan (ed.). *The Last Voyage*. London: Harvill, 1997.

Stevenson, Randall. *The British Novel since the Thirties*. London: Batsford, 1986.

Sutherland, John. *The Macmillan Guide to Victorian Fiction*. London: Macmillan, 1980.

Taylor, A. J. P. *English History 1914–1945*. London: Penguin, 1975.

Thomas, M. Wynn. *Corresponding Cultures*. Cardiff: University of Wales Press, 1999.

Trezise, Simon. *The West Country as a Literary Invention*. Exeter, U.K.: Exeter University Press, 2000.

Trinder, Barrie. *A History of Shropshire*. London: Phillimore, 1983.

Wade, Stephen (ed.). *Gladsongs and Gatherings*. Liverpool: Liverpool University Press, 2001.

Wheeler, Michael. *English Fiction of the Victorian Period*. London: Longmans, 1985.

Williams, Raymond. *Writing in Society*. Cambridge: Verso, 1989.

Essays in Journals and Collections

Andrews, William. "James Burnley." In Charles Forshaw (ed.), *The Poets of Keighley, Bingley and Howarth*. Bradford, U.K.: Thornton and Pearson, 1891.

Barker, Paul. "Review of Stan Barstow, *In My Own Time*." *Times Literary Supplement*, 11 January 2002.

Berridge, Elizabeth. "Notes from the Boilerhouse." *London Magazine,* December 1999.

Calder-Marshall, Arthur. "Fiction." *Fact*, 15 July 1937.

Chapman, Raymond. "A True Representation: Speech in the Novels of Thomas Hardy." In Beatrice White (ed.), *Essays and Studies*. London: John Murray, 1983.

Crawford, Tom. "Introduction." In Lewis Grassic Gibbon, *A Scots Quair*. Edinburgh: Canongate, 1995.

Hamilton, Ian. "The Making of the Movement." In M. Schmidt & Grevel Lindop (eds.), *British Poetry since 1970*. Manchester, U.K.: Carcanet, 1972.

Harris, John. "Introduction." In Caradoc Evans, *My People*. Bridgend, U.K.: Seren, 1987.

Kiberd, Declan. "Irish Literature and Irish History." In R. F. Foster, *The Oxford History of Ireland*. Oxford: Oxford University Press, 1989.

Maxwell, Ian. "Highland Clearances." *Family History*, 72, September 2001.

Morgan, Prys. "From a Death to a View: The Hunt for the Welsh Past in the Romantic Period." In Philip Hobsbawn and Terence Ranger, *The Invention of Tradition*. Cambridge: Canto, 1983.

Norris, Margot. "The Lethal Turn of the Twentieth Century." In Robert Newman (ed.), *Centuries, Ends, Narratives, Means*. Cambridge: Cambridge University Press 1998.

Pick, J. B. "Introduction." Neil Gunn, *The Key of the Chest*. Edinburgh: Canongate, 1998.

Pringle, Trevor, R. "The Privation of History: Landseer, Victoria and the Highland Myth." In Denis Cosgrove and Stephen Daniels (eds.), *The Iconography of Landscape*. Cambridge: Cambridge University Press, 1988.

Roberts, Lewis C. "Disciplining and Disinfecting Working-Class Readers in the Victorian Public Library." In *Victorian Literature and Culture*, 26 (1998): 105–132.

Swinnerton, Frank. "Introduction." In Arnold Bennett, *Anna of the Five Towns*. London: Penguin, 1954.

Thomas, David N. "Under Milk Wood's Birth in Exile." *New Welsh Review*, 52 (2000): 47–53.

Young, Robin. "Outsider Figures in Nineteenth Century Poetry." In H. W. Ludwig and Lothar Fietz, *Poetry in the British Isles: Non-Metropolitan Perspectives*. Cardiff: University of Wales Press, 1995.

Index

About the Author

STEPHEN WADE is a Senior Lecturer in English at the University of Huddersfield, England. He has published several scholarly books and articles, as well as some collections of poems.